Ghost Stories

of

Philadelphia, PA

Ghost Stories

of

Philadelphia, PA

by Tim Reeser

GHOST STORIES OF PHILADELPHIA, PA

Second Printing 2008
Printed in the United States of America
ISBN: 0-9729265-4-2

For Eileen,

the Ghost Lady of Philadelphia

Front Cover:

WAYNE

VINING

ROSS

CONWELL

GRATZ

PHYSICK

LOGAN

LAFAYETTE

BLAVATZKY

DONWELL

ARNOLD

WHITE

ANDRE

SHIPPEN

Ghost Stories of Philadelphia, PA

Contents

Concealed in the shadows of history, hiding among folklore and legend, live the tales of ghosts, haunted houses and spirits that lurk in the dark. Bequeathed from generation to generation, whispered so as not to wake the dead, these tales endure the passage of time — refusing to go quietly into the night.

Philadelphia's folklore, or more aptly — ghostlore — reaches back centuries, but new hauntings continue to materialize. Ghostlore offers a fascinating depiction of superstition and belief in the supernatural, exposing people's fears and in some cases their salvation. The stories collected in this book come from a variety of sources. Some are old tales enhanced here with new information or insight; others are told for the first time ever.

The impetus behind the book lies with the Ghost Tour of Philadelphia, a candlelight walking tour that brings history back to life — in the *most haunted city in America*!

Independence Square
Manifest Destiny

No other set of buildings in "America's most haunted city" better deserves the title of "the most haunted" than those on Independence Square at Chestnut Street between 5th and 6th Streets. Commonly referred to as the birthplace of the United States, their hallowed halls safeguarded representatives from the thirteen British colonies in America while they crafted a new nation — declaring their independence in 1776.

Of the famous Americans who participated in that bold venture, it would surprise no one to hear that the ghosts of the venerable Benjamin Franklin, the stoic George Washington, the passionate John Adams and the scholarly Thomas Jefferson still roam its hallways or haunt its chambers. But conversely, as numerous as are the tales of supernatural activity inside the complex of buildings once known as State House Row, little evidence exists to identify the capricious spirits that haunt its ancient hallways and chambers.

Independence Hall and its companion buildings, Old City Hall, on the east side at 5th and Chestnut, and Congress Hall, on the west side at 6th and Chestnut, are seperated by the East Wing and West Wing respectively. Long before the history-making drama of forming a new country and before the name Independence Hall existed, the buildings served in the rather mundane capacity as the governing center of the Province of Pennsylvania. But, starting with the events leading up to the Revolutionary War, its destiny and identity forever changed, and the magnitude of its significance as an American icon remains unparalleled.

Despite the site's well-documented history as a seat of government and its heralded roll in founding a new nation, the various buildings served in a multitude of capacities ... some with grim consequences.

During the Revolution, when the British occupied Philadelphia, the upper gallery served as a hospital for wounded soldiers. According to *Life and Times in Colonial Philadelphia,* after the British retreated from the city, Philadelphians complained about "the offensiveness of the air in and around the State House, which the Enemy had made an Hospital and left it in a condition disgraceful to the Character of civility. Particularly they had opened a large square pit near the House, a receptacle for filth, into which there they had also cast dead horses and the bodies of men who by the mercy of death had escaped from their further cruelties."

COURTESY LIBRARY OF CONGRESS

Makeshift hospital during the Revolution

In the yellow fever epidemic of 1793, the Pennsylvania legislature suspended meetings in August after the doorman, Joseph Fry, died of the malady in his apartment in the West Wing. Undertakers also took to selling coffins from the 5th Street corner outside the building and "let their horses eat oats from the crudely constructed wooden boxes."

COURTESY LIBRARY OF CONGRESS

West Wing

During the extended Abraham Lincoln funeral procession of 1865, the assassinated president lay in state in the Assembly Room on the first floor on the east side of the building.

More recently, in a 1968 excavation of a pit found in the alley between the East Wing and Old City Hall, researchers "found human remains, including pieces of skull and arm bones ..." Whispers of medical experiments and cadaver trafficking began after medicine bottles from a nearby druggist, known for unsavory dealings with the dead, were also found among the human remains.

The East Wing and Old City Hall, site of a macabre find.

COURTESY LIBRARY OF CONGRESS

Could the historic site's use as a make-shift hospital, the death of Joseph Fry, the "pit" of dead men and horses, and the possibility of cadaver trafficking be the cause of the paranormal activity at Independence Hall?

From *DIGESTezine*, an internet magazine featuring haunted tales of Philadelphia, comes a story from 1943. On a cold snowy November night at about 2:00 a.m., a security guard, alone in quiet solitude, heard the door leading to the chamber where the Declaration of Independence was signed, slowly open and a low moan emanate from the darkness. Reportedly, he never returned to work after that night.

In 1994, a historical tour guide claimed to have witnessed the apparition of a solder from colonial times filter through the front door and disappear.

Has anyone seen the doorman?

Finally, from a 2002 interview with two park rangers, both of whom confirmed unexplainable encounters within Independence Hall, comes the tale of an invisible intruder ... invisible at least, to them. In the middle of the night, their radios crackled, "Breach of security at Independence Hall." The pair rushed in, searched the chambers and galleries from top to bottom but found no one. They radioed back, "All clear." But something continued to trigger the alarm, and headquarters radioed, "No! Someone is in there — go back in!" They repeated the search and again came up empty, and again repeated the all clear signal. Completely exasperated, the ranger at headquarters responded, "I'm looking at you on the monitor ... there's a man standing right next to you!" They looked around, saw nobody and wasted no time exiting the building.

The iconic buildings of Independence Square have survived through peace and war, fame and obscurity, neglect and abuse to become the spiritual crossroad of American freedom. That legacy still manifests ... in ways we may not completely understand!

Rappings, tappings, & footsteps from the Ghost Tour of Philadelphia!

November 2001 — A park ranger approached a tour guide and asked if Congress Hall was on the tour because, in his opinion, it was definitely haunted. He then shared a recent experience. As he was leaving Congress Hall after a security check, he received a call that the monitors had picked up activity inside. He went back in and discovered all the cabinet doors wide open when, just a minute before, they were closed. He added that it was common to smell cigar smoke on the second floor even when the building was empty. He said the empty buildings of Independence Square "creeped him out," and a short while later, he transferred to Valley Forge.

July 7, 2004 — Eileen approached four park rangers and asked if they had any new ghost stories — they all laughed. One of them opened up by nervously saying he had heard things about Old City Hall. His coworkers laughed at him, but he continued anyway: "No, seriously, that place is eerie." He said that sometimes while on break, rangers will take a short nap upstairs. Many have said that as soon as they fall asleep they have a terrible nightmare that wakes them. So unnerving is this dream that they are unable to fall back to sleep. By the end of his tale, the other rangers were nodding their heads and agreeing that they too had heard the loud banging noises and footsteps while alone in Old City Hall.

New City Tavern

City Tavern
Resurrection

City Tavern, one of Philadelphia's early colonial eateries frequented by many of our famous forefathers, continues to serve and attract patrons as it did more than 200 years ago. Prominently located at the corner of 2nd and Walnut Streets, the rebuilt landmark closely resembles the structure built in 1773 when the British still ruled the American colonies.

Among the notable Americans who frequented City Tavern were George Washington, Thomas Jefferson, Benjamin Franklin, John Adams and many other patriots who came to eat, drink and talk. City Tavern served not only sustenance for the body, but also intellectual sustenance for those early revolutionaries in search of open-minded discussions on the structure and principles of a new republic, free from the tyranny of the British crown.

But with the stories of historic significance that emanate from one of Philadelphia's most indelible institutions come tales of supernatural phenomena caused by several macabre events.

A former general manager of City Tavern attributes many of the ghost sightings to the violence that erupted inside City Tavern in 1781. Customers and employees alike have witnessed the appearance of a late night specter. He materializes in the bar room with an anguished, pleading look on his face, before slumping to the floor and vanishing. Described as wearing a white colonial-era shirt with a bloodstained chest, the apparition, many believe, belongs to a City Tavern waiter killed by a Revolutionary soldier.

Appropriately enough, Mad Anthony Wayne plays a crucial role in the story, adding to his

Legend has it that at one time, duels were held behind City Tavern to settle disputes.

legacy of seemingly having left behind a ghost story wherever he traveled.

A probable cause for the reputed accidental and tragic incident lies in the events surrounding Wayne's men during a difficult period of time for American troops during the Revolution.

Late in the year of 1780, Wayne and his troops were wintering in New Jersey. The outcome of the war with England remained undecided, and the American forces were in sad shape. Wayne's troops, like many in the grueling war for independence, were short of food, clothing and shelter. When the Continental Congress refused to authorize funds for the long overdue pay of the enlistees and instead diverted payment to new recruits, a mutiny broke out.

After a rowdy and rambunctious night of drinking-in the New Year of 1781, a sizable number of Wayne's men decided to march to Philadelphia and demand their pay from Congress. Wayne's efforts to stop the insurrection failed, although he did persuade them to halt near Trenton and reconsider their fractious scheme, giving him time to travel to Philadelphia to lobby Congress on their behalf.

Upon arriving in Philadelphia, Wayne and several members of his command visited City Tavern, not only for refreshment, but also for information. Many delegates from Congress and other influential people frequented the tavern, and it became the unofficial nerve center of the war.

Sometime during their visit, an argument broke out between several patrons and Wayne's men, which then escalated into a drunken brawl. Although the reason for the melee remains undocumented, perhaps arguments or comments regarding the seditious actions of Wayne's troops precipitated the incident. In the confusion, a City Tavern waiter, whose name remains lost to history, lay bleeding — mortally wounded.

Apparition in the Bar Room?

One of Wayne's men, Colonel Craig, stood accused of the deed. As the stricken server lay bleeding with a wound to his chest, the authorities were summoned. Before they arrived, Wayne hustled the killer off, hiding him in a closet in the basement of City Tavern until Wayne could smuggle him out of town back to camp.

> *...a drunken brawl involving American officers led to the murder of a waiter, and General Anthony Wayne shielded the suspect from the searching constabulary.*
> *- Life and Times in Colonial Philadelphia*

As callous as it may sound, innocent people are frequently killed during moments of violence, and throughout history those moments are well-known for leaving behind an everlasting supernatural imprint that manifests over and over, usually in the form of the victims' apparitions seeking retribution.

Perhaps that long-ago City Tavern waiter, whose killer escaped to live his life to its fullest, spends the afterlife obsessed with finding the justice denied him at his time of death.

> *Colonel Craig played a critical role in a key episode of the war, earning near-hero status, as documented in family archives: "[He] was at Valley Forge in the winter of 1777-78, and it was through him that Mrs. Lydia Darrach, conveyed to Washington that warning of Howe's expected attack at Whitemarsh… He died, Jan 13, 1832, aged 92 years, and was buried with military and masonic honors."*
>
> *— Craig family archives*

Another well-known and oft-told story of paranormal activity at City Tavern involves a tale of unrequited love, sudden catastrophe and tragic death.

In 1854, during preparations for a wedding at City Tavern, a fire swept through the building with tragic consequences. The fire started on the second floor where the bride-to-be, attended to by her bridesmaids, primped and prepared for the big event.

Unnoticed in the hub-bub and excitement, a fire broke out and quickly engulfed the upstairs. Some surmise that the bride's dress, described as exquisite with a train ten feet long, first caught fire, and in their frenzy to extinguish the flames, the bride and her attendants lost valuable time to save themselves as the fire quickly spread.

Yesteryear's ballroom, today's dining room

Downstairs the groom waited in the pub with his attendants, perhaps a drink or two taken to calm the nerves before the big event, when screams and thick black smoke suddenly came bellowing from above. Trapped by the heat and flames and overcome by the thick smoke, some members of the wedding party perished, including the bride. A day that started as one of hope with promise to the future ended in tragedy and loss.

Later that year, due to damage from the wedding-day fire, City Tavern itself became a memory when the ruins were demolished.

But in 1975, in preparation for the Bicentennial celebration, a new City Tavern opened. Rebuilt to its original specifications, City Tavern offers the same epicurean services to Philadelphia's visitors as it did two centuries ago – a place for good food, good drink and perhaps a spirited encounter!

> "Modern-day City Tavern staff swear there's a ghost in the restaurant – table settings are moved, dishes come crashing off the wall. Who knows? Maybe it's the nameless waiter murdered in the original City Tavern by Col. Craig on January 3, 1781 after a drunken brawl. The murder was never prosecuted, some say because of the class differences that separated the two men."
> — *City Tavern Cookbook*

Evidently, more than just a colonial era replica was resurrected. On occasion, guests at City Tavern report the manifestation of a misty mournful woman dressed in a wedding gown on the staircase to the second floor. Reportedly, she sometimes appears in photographs taken during wedding celebrations ... an uninvited guest whose phantom image appears in the background still young of face and dressed in a white gown. Affectionately dubbed the "Bride of City Tavern," she seems intent on experiencing that most special of events, one she never experienced in the flesh, and, despite her horrific death, one she does not mind sharing with the living!

Old City Tavern

Rappings, tappings, & footsteps from the Ghost Tour of Philadelphia!

May 2001
While waiting for the tour to start, tour guides Mickey and Eileen struck up a conversation with Jay, a park ranger. He claimed that just about all the park buildings are haunted. To prove to a fellow ranger that City Tavern was haunted, Jay took him late at night after everyone had gone. They walked to the top floor and back down to make sure no one was in the building and then waited quietly. Several minutes later the intrepid ghost hunters heard footsteps directly overhead but upon searching again found no one.

May 2001 (inside City Tavern)
Tour guide Mickey asked George, the manager, about his experiences at the Tavern. George said it's not unusual to hear footsteps in empty parts of the building after they've closed for the evening. Usually the last to leave, he was in his third floor office one night when he heard what sounded like furniture being moved downstairs. In a downstairs room he found all the chairs moved to one

side of the room. He also claimed to have witnessed the apparition of a woman in the long hall.

Visions of the afterlife!

Temple University
Test of Faith

One of Philadelphia's most well-known citizens at the turn of the 20th century left a legacy that still endures today despite his apparent obscurity in the collective consciousness. Reverend Russell Conwell came to Philadelphia in the early 1880s on a divine mission and by all accounts over-achieved.

Starting out at the tiny Grace Baptist Church on Berks Street, Conwell utilized his dynamic talent as an orator to further his civic accomplishments, including the founding of Temple University. The school's main campus, situated on North Broad Street, still retains remnants of the Conwell era, including his onetime home, the historic Baptist Temple church and the memorialized remains of Conwell and his wife Sarah in the Founders Garden.

Perhaps best-known during his lifetime for his talent as a public orator, Conwell's speaking engagements led him around the country. In his prime, Conwell averaged 200 speeches per year.

Early Poster

Conwell's most famous speech, a parable called "Acres of Diamonds" that he presented more than 6000 times, tells the tale of the riches to be found in one's own backyard, and according to his biographer, "...to come under his eloquence and the swelling resonance of his voice...was to receive a spiritual illumination."

Conwell's calling in life took a meandering path through a variety of jobs, including lawyer, lecturer, newspaper editor and writer, among others, before he finally settled on that of a minister.

His spiritual enlightenment emerged during the Civil War, when a traumatic event spurred his interest in Spiritism — the ability to communicate with the dead — a practice he admitted to frequently after his wife of thirty-six years, Sarah, died in 1910. His home at 2020 North Broad Street served as the scene for many of these dreamy encounters with his beloved wife.

A Russell Conwell metaphor on life and death: "... I quit life as I would an inn... I shall check out and go to meet my next engagement... and start on the last and greatest and most thrilling trip of all... My bags are packed, my friends have gone ahead. I shall be going to those I love... leaving the inn and going home."

But Russell Conwell's rise to prominence began when he left Yale University and enlisted in the Union Army during the Civil War. Having already established himself as an influential and talented public speaker, he used that talent to recruit young men from his area of Massachusetts to enlist in the army.

Conwell with sword

Conwell's popularity and obvious leadership qualities led to his commission as Captain of his unit. In a show of honor and devotion, Conwell's men purchased a new sword for him. Not just any sword, but a gilded ornamented sword engraved in Latin with "True Friendship is Eternal."

This sword and one particular member of Conwell's unit would transform Conwell from an atheist to a "man of God." Johnny Ring, from Conwell's hometown, joined the unit as Conwell's personal aide. Despite his small, frail stature, Johnny displayed a remarkable amount of courage in the midst of a surprise attack by the Confederates. Conwell attributed his spiritual awakening to that day and the heroics of Johnny Ring. In 1915, Conwell painted a vivid memory of the moment for his biographer, Robert Shackleton:

"... The scabbard of the sword was too glittering for the regulations and I could not wear it, and could only wear a plain one for service and keep this hanging in my tent on the tent-pole. John Ring used to handle it adoringly, and kept it polished to brilliancy.

One day the Confederates suddenly stormed our position ... all ... retreated hurriedly across the river, setting fire to a long wooden bridge as we went over. It soon blazed up furiously, making a barrier that the Confederates could not pass.

But, unknown to everybody, and unnoticed, John Ring had dashed back to my tent … and took down, from where it was hanging on the tent-pole, my bright, gold-scabbarded sword.

… He dodged here and there, and actually managed to gain the bridge just as it was beginning to blaze … The flames were every moment getting fiercer, the smoke denser, and now and then, as he crawled and staggered on, he leaned for a few seconds far over the edge of the bridge in an effort to get air … both sides watched his terrible progress … And then a Confederate officer--he was one of General Pickett's officers--ran to the water's edge and waved a white handkerchief and the firing ceased.

'Tell that boy … to come back here and we will let him go free!'

The roar of the flames was so close to Ring that he could not hear the calls from either side of the river, and he pushed desperately on and disappeared in the covered part.

There was dead silence … All waited in hopeless expectancy. And then came a mighty yell from Northerner and Southerner alike, for Johnnie came crawling out … and his clothes were ablaze, and he toppled over and fell into shallow water; and in a few moments he was dragged out, unconscious, and hurried to a hospital.

He lingered for a day or so, still unconscious, and then came to himself and smiled a little as he found that the sword for which he had given his life had been left beside him. He took it in his arms. He hugged it to his breast. He gave a few words of final message for me. And that was all."

Johnny Ring's devotion and death defying heroics haunted Conwell and caused him to rethink his place and purpose on Earth. He vowed to live two lives — one Johnny Ring's, the other his — and committed to work sixteen hours a day, eight for Johnny, the other eight his own.

Conwell rose to Colonel in the army, survived a serious battlefield wound and after the war returned to Massachusetts. He kept the sword for which Johnny gave his life hanging over his bed, and every morning, he would gaze at that sword, and recommit himself to the work that lay ahead of him.

Did Conwell communicate with Johnny Ring's spirit? Conwell's belief in Spiritism and devotion to Johnny

Ring's memory implies the possibility, despite the lack of documentation confirming those encounters.

Clearly, however, according to an article published in *American Magazine* in 1921, Conwell did communicate with his dead wife's spirit following her death in 1910 from cancer.

Sarah Conwell arrived in Philadelphia with Russell and became active in his ventures, playing an instrumental role in the development and nourishment of the Baptist church, Temple College and the Samaritan Hospital.

Grace Temple Baptist Church

By all accounts Russell and Sarah were soul-mates, and she participated in the development of these institutions more as a business partner than a wife. Her passing left a huge gap in Russell's personal and professional life. Admittedly, he missed her immensely.

Russell   Sarah

Shortly after her death, Russell dreamt that Sarah appeared to him at the foot of their bed smiling pleasantly. The "dream" kept recurring, and although he mentioned it to no one, he began to talk with her. Despite her lifelike appearance and engaging conversations, Russell feared that his mourning at her loss had made him delusional. So he contrived a test, both for his sanity and his interest in psychic phenomena.

One morning, according to the article, Russell said to the specter, "I know you aren't really there."

"Oh, but I am!" she replied.

"But how can I be sure? Are you willing that I should test you?" She nodded and with a smile disappeared.

The next morning Sarah appeared at her accustomed time and location, and Russell went right to the exam. "Tell me then, where are my army discharge papers?" Russell had not seen the papers in quite awhile, but he knew they were somewhere in the house.

Without hesitating, Sarah answered, "Why, they are in the black japanned box behind the books in your library." Russell jumped out of bed and rushed to the library, and after searching the shelves, he found the box behind a row of books and his discharge papers tucked underneath.

Sarah appeared again the next morning with a satisfied "I told you so" look on her face, but Russell remained unconvinced. He asked her if she would perform another test and, with a great smile of enthusiasm, she agreed before disappearing.

At breakfast that morning, Russell asked Mary, one of the maids who had been with him for many years, to hide a fountain pen that he had received from Sarah before her death. He instructed her not to tell him or anyone else where she put it.

As the next day dawned, Sarah appeared once again, anxiously awaiting the next test. Russell asked, "Do you know where Mary hid my pen?" She laughed, "Of course I do. Get out of bed and come with me."

Russell did as she said, and holding his hand she led him to the closet in his room. Sarah pointed to the top of the closet, and Russell stood on a chair as he felt around the top shelf of the closet. Unable to find the pen, he went to step down, certain that indeed his mind teetered on the verge of insanity. But Sarah, standing in the doorway of the closet, shaking her head, stopped him and imploringly pointed to the top of the closet again. Russell searched again, stretching as far as he could to reach the very back of the closet, and there to his amazement, he found the pen.

Conwell's death notice was quite clear on his belief in psychic phenomena: "...the psychic tenants of his old age were expressed with quiet conviction, which provoked no opposition."

Perhaps because of his non-secular reputation and devotion to Christianity, Conwell initially hesitated in publicizing the encounter with his dead wife. But a man of such strong convictions trusts himself and what he believes above all else, and eventually, Conwell began to share the unusual incident, treating it as a matter of fact, not to be disputed.

Inspired and faithful to the memory of Johnny Ring throughout his life, devoted to his ministry and wife to the end, Russell Conwell undoubtedly believed that *true friendship is eternal!*

"I See Dead People"

Spiritism was the underlying theme to the widely popular movie "The Sixth Sense," produced by local filmmaker M. Night Shamalan. Several scenes were filmed in Philadelphia.

Bizarre Halloween
Portals of Terror

Philadelphia, PA
October 31, 1998
A bizarre and unexplainable set of circumstances left the staff of a commercial Halloween event shaking their heads in bewilderment. On the spookiest night of the year, when witches take to the sky, the dead rise from the grave, spells are cast and black cats shunned, real live ghosts appeared to frighten the bejeezus out of workers at two Halloween events. According to the *victims*, the phenomena occurred at the exact same moment despite miles of distance between the events...

This unusual report of paranormal activity appeared in the *Sixpenny Chronicles*, an eclectic periodical featuring extraordinary phenomena.

First-hand accounts of the strange events that transpired that Halloween night centered on paranormal encounters at two of Philadelphia's most imposing, gothic-like historic structures: Eastern State Penitentiary, located at 22nd Street and Fairmount Avenue, and Fort Mifflin, on Hog Island Road near the Philadelphia airport.

Since the mid-1990s, Eastern State Penitentiary morphs every October into one of the city's premier Halloween events, with costumed actors and elaborate sets erected inside its old stone walls. Known as "Terror Behind the Walls," it provides the ultimate dark fantasy of confinement, terror and escape in a make-believe Halloween atmosphere.

COURTESY LIBRARY OF CONGRESS

Receiving its first prisoner in 1829 and in use until 1971, Eastern State Penitentiary became notorious for its inhumane use of solitary confinement.

In 1998, Fort Mifflin participated in the "Terror Behind the Walls" production with its own intricately decorated casemates and outlandishly attired actors, creating a spectacular two-part Halloween venue.

Originally built by the British in 1771, then abandoned before the Revolution, the fort was commandeered by the Americans under Benjamin Franklin in 1776.

In preparation for the Halloween season, the production crew maniacally scavenged several old warehouses in Fishtown and Hunting Park for props. Fortuitously, they stumbled upon an abandoned warehouse containing decades of old statuary and design sets that added grotesque and surreal touches to the normally somber prison and fort. Encased in huge monolithic stone walls guarded by huge, heavy, securely locking doors, these unfamiliar places added a certain fear-factor to the entire notion of traipsing through darkness. Besides, according to legend, both the prison and the fort were haunted, adding a bit of realism to the manufactured horror.

In 1998, both properties operated independently as historic tourist attractions, and the production company decided to interview the employees for the purpose of integrating the site's haunted history into the Halloween event.

In a place where locks and keys keep the "bogie-man" sequestered from the public, it seems ironic that the Penitentiary's scrape with the supernatural comes from their locksmith. He told a discombobulated tale, where hundreds of anguished spirits shrouded in a bilious vapor pursued him in a phantasmagoria of epic proportions. Chased out of the prison by the tortured souls of, presumably, former prisoners, the locksmith ran for his life to the safety of the gate-keeper station. Another vague tale of crying babies in the women's cellblock adds to the creepy ambiance of the abandoned and derelict prison.

In 1842, Charles Dickens wrote a scathing report on the horrible conditions at Eastern State. After interviewing a prisoner he wrote: "he is like a man buried alive; to be dug out in the slow round of years; and in the meantime dead to everything but torturing anxieties and horrible despair."

Fort Mifflin's haunted history, richly detailed and well documented in various books and publications, include the "screaming woman," the long-ago officer's wife who hung herself after her daughter died of typhoid fever, the Civil War prisoner convicted of murder and hanged in the courtyard, "the man with no face" and several more. The abundance of sightings and supernatural incidents lead some to believe the fort may serve as a portal, a passageway between other dimensions and the physical world.

Although undaunted by the plethora of hauntings, the production crew at both locations shared a certain apprehensiveness. Would something go wrong? Were poltergeists lurking, ready to unleash chaos? One artist, after just a single day at the prison, refused to return, claiming he could not work in a place infested with so much evil. Several actors refused to work alone, not because they saw anything otherworldly, but because of an overwhelming feeling of dread, as if at any moment something terrible might happen. Fortunately, however, the Halloween event ran smoothly, and reports of supernatural phenomena never materialized until the last night ... Halloween.

Saturday nights draw the largest crowds to most Halloween events, and the largest of the largest occurs when the annual holy night of terror falls on a Saturday. In this particular year, Halloween fell on a Saturday, and the fort and the prison were expecting extraordinary crowds.

> *Halloween: Celtic festival of the dead... called Samhain... It was the biggest and most significant holiday of the Celtic year. The Celts believed that at the time of Samhain, more so than any other time of the year, the ghosts of the dead were able to mingle with the living...*
> — www.loc.gov

Perhaps the huge number of people, the elevated energy level and the excitement of Halloween explains what happened that night — or maybe it was something else.

But the lack of supernatural intervention was about to end.

The site manager for the Halloween event at Eastern State Penitentiary, Jim, explained, "It was about 11:00; the place was really rocking, big crowd, high energy. My two-way radio beeps and security says there's a problem in cellblock six. The actors have stopped working, and they're huddled together in the middle of the cellblock." Jim made his way to the trouble area and found six actors gathered in one spot with uncertain, frightened looks on their faces. Pointing to the end of the cellblock, they claimed to have seen the ghost of a man dressed in uniform — not just once but several times. The apparition materialized at the door of the very last cell, peered inside, and then walked to the next cell where he disappeared.

Jim had worked closely with all six during the event and knew them well. "They were really scared," he said. "They believed they saw something down there." Jim stayed with the rattled crew awhile but never saw anything unusual. Still frightened, the actors refused to return to that end of the cellblock, and Jim re-positioned them to other areas.

Haunted cellblock!

Meanwhile, at Fort Mifflin, the huge crowd snaked its way through the old buildings and dome-ceilinged casemates in a Halloween frenzy. Ron, event site manager at the Fort, frantically bounced around from set to set, substituting actors, tweaking special effects and managing to keep his wits about him in the general mayhem of a crazy night.

Having delved into every nook and cranny of the fort during the two months of setting up for Halloween and then managing the event, Ron had become familiar with nuances of light and sound inside the strange catacomb-like structure of casemates in the northeast corner of the fort.

Voices from the other side!

As he hurried through the complex of casemates, Ron heard something: "I was in the catacombs walking by the room we used for storage and that nobody was allowed into. As I passed by, I heard voices, not just whispers, but normal sounding voices, as if a conversation was going on. I expected to find some actors in there, goofing off, taking a break. I threw open the door, ready to get on them for being there, but when I looked ... there wasn't a soul around. Shivers ran up the back of my neck."

So life-like were the voices, Ron remained convinced that he had heard "voices from the other side."

Later, while Ron and Jim swapped the night's stories, they realized that the weird encounters at the prison and fort occurred at the same time, even though miles apart.

The October transformation from staid historic monuments into creepy, forbidding "haunted houses" attracted thousands of thrill-seeking, scare-me-if-you-can customers that year, and circumstances being what they were, some otherworldly attraction occurred as well.

The _Six Penny Chronicles_ reported on a similar incident on the same night at the Lizzie Lincoln Haunted House in Birdsboro, Pennsylvania. Just before midnight, two actors were frightened by a female apparition that descended the attic staircase. And like the actors at Eastern State Penitentiary, they abandoned their work stations.

Betsy Ross House circa 2007

Betsy Ross House
Secrets, Lies & Legends

Another of Philadelphia's icons that strays into the world of the paranormal involves the legendary Elizabeth Griscom, canonized as Betsy Ross. The building at 239 Arch Street, known as the Betsy Ross House, rates as one of the most popular tourist attractions in the city and as a must see for out-of-town visitors. In addition to its place in history, the quaint old building that dates back to the 1700s holds a few secrets you will not hear on a tour of the Betsy Ross House.

Particularly the one concerning an ethereal Betsy who appears weeping at the foot of a bed in an upstairs bedroom, or the one involving a murky shadow of a shooting victim said to haunt the claustrophobia inducing cellar.

The Betsy Ross legend itself remains controversial, plagued with distorted facts, whispered innuendos and unsolved mysteries that compel scholars and folklorists alike to periodically examine and re-examine this ancient lady's life and ... her *afterlife*.

Betsy's ancestors were some of the earliest settlers of New Jersey and Philadelphia. The family patriarch, Betsy's great-grandfather Andrew Griscom, arrived in New Jersey in the early 1680s, about the same time William Penn established his Philadelphia haven for religious freedom and social equality. Andrew purchased a large tract of land in New Jersey and approximately 500 acres on the edge of the infant town of Philadelphia in the area now known as the Spring Garden district.

According to Griscom family archives, Andrew arrived in America already a wealthy man at the age of twenty. The source of his wealth remains a mystery, but some believe that it derived from his father, Jack Griscom, an alleged pirate who prowled and plundered the waters of the new world during the mid 1600s. Family folklore suggests that Jack paid for his misdeeds at the end of a hangman's noose, and that his nefarious occupation provided son Andrew with the money to stake his claim in the British colonies of New Jersey and Pennsylvania.

"Unknown to many genealogists, the existence of Jack Griscom was discovered by the novelist, James Michener, while researching his novel 'Chesapeake.' Jack Griscom was a pirate who, with Henry Bonfleur, had pretended to be Welsh Quakers while scouting out the settlements of America in the late 1660's. He... had at least one child, Andrew Griscom... Jack Griscom was shot to death in St. Lucie and his booty never recovered. The Michener reference is the only one leading to a Jack Griscom, no other information on him has been found." –genealogy.com

Ambitious and hardworking, Andrew Griscom thrived as a skilled craftsman in early Philadelphia and earned distinction for building the first brick home in the new town. His grandsons followed in his footsteps, including Betsy's father Samuel, who participated in building Independence Hall and in the founding of Carpenters' Hall.

Although they established a reputation as one of Philadelphia's prominent colonial-era families, there nevertheless existed in the Griscom family legacy a streak of rebelliousness and individualism that periodically led to scandal and heresy.

Betsy's parents, raised as Quakers, defied church protocol with their disreputable behavior. Accused of "unchaste intimacy before marriage," the couple faced expulsion from the church, but upon showing repentance they remained as members in good standing for the remainder of their lives. Betsy deviated from the accepted code of conduct as well, with completely different consequences.

> *The Betsy Ross story never proved popular with Hollywood, although two early silent films were produced:*
> *Betsy Ross in 1917 starring Alice Brady and The Flag in 1927 starring Enid Bennett.*

A middle child in a brood of seventeen siblings, Betsy exhibited skill as a seamstress while still a teenager. Described as petite with captivating blue eyes and a lively disposition, she was known for her fierce temperament, qualities that young gentlemen of that period found irresistible. As the story goes, three local men were anxious to court Betsy, John Ross, Joseph Ashburn and John Claypoole. And as strange as it seems, she would eventually marry all three.

While apprenticing at Webster's upholstery shop on 2nd Street, Betsy became enchanted with fellow apprentice John Ross, scion of a distinguished Philadelphia family. Against all convention, and church rules, John and Betsy eloped to Gloucester, New Jersey on the other side of the Delaware River where they exchanged vows at Hugg's Tavern.

The fact that her new husband did not belong to the Quaker faith made the union doubly reproachful, and once again a Griscom appeared in the Quaker Book of Discipline accused of "Mixing in Marriage with those not of our Profession." Expelled from her family's church, an unrepentant Betsy attended services at the Episcopalian Christ Church where the Ross family worshiped.

Outcast, but stubborn, the young Betsy and John Ross persevered and established their own upholstery shop in a small building on Arch Street.

Betsy, however, apparently had other skills in addition to those of a seamstress. Family archives indicate that Betsy practiced as a healer, and whispers of witchcraft circulated around her use of herbs. In an era when the practice of medicine sometimes carried an aura of magic, such innuendos were not uncommon. Surprisingly, she also carried the gift of clairvoyance, the ability to foretell future events.

Some people question Betsy's relationship with George Washington as it pertains to the flag-making legend. With her aptitude for predicting future events, and Washington a believer in divine providence, did she serve as a prognosticator as well as a seamstress?

Despite Betsy's extraordinary talents, bad luck and tragedy seemed to plague her matrimonial life. American history books state that John Ross died in an explosion while guarding the docks along the Philadelphia waterfront during the Revolutionary War. Griscom family lore suggests that John Ross succumbed to insanity, just as his mother had, brought on perhaps from handling chemical concoctions while working as an upholsterer. John suffered for 18 months with his malady, finally perishing after barely two years of marriage. At the time of John's death, according to family archives, the star-crossed coupled lived in the house next to the modern-day Betsy Ross House.

Undoubtedly Betsy faced tremendous adversity at this point in her life — disconnected from her support network of family and church after excommunication from the Quakers while nursing a dying husband as he slowly lost his mind. Betsy somehow kept going, trying to support herself with the upholstery shop, struggling on just as her new country struggled with the uncertainty and horrors of war with England.

Betsy and the birth of the American Flag

After John's own prolonged struggle ended, Betsy relocated next door where the well-known legend of the American Flag unfolded. Three wise-men from the Continental Congress paid a historic visit to Betsy's house on Arch Street. The triumvirate consisted of the most powerful Americans of their time, George Washington, her dead husband's uncle, George Ross, and financier Robert Morris. They blessed the birth of the nation's flag by the widowed patriot after she convinced them to forego the six-sided star for the easier to make five-sided star. Legends are always steeped in symbolism, but according to Betsy's ancestors and despite some inaccuracies, this legend matches closely with the story passed down from generation to generation.

> During a 2007 tour of the Betsy Ross House, a Betsy reenactor demonstrated the simple technique for making a 5-point star with one snip of the scissors. She also demonstrated a similarly simple technique for making a 6-point star with a single snip.

The year after John Ross' death, Betsy married previous suitor Joseph Ashburn. But this marriage seemed cursed as well, as circumstances and history intervened with another fatal blow to Betsy. Ashburn spent much of his time at sea in service of the newly formed United States of America, and shortly after setting sail on a privateering mission, Ashburn and his crew were captured by the British and banished to a notorious prison in England. By an odd coincidence, Ashburn found himself imprisoned with an old friend from Philadelphia, John Claypoole, yet another former Betsy pursuer, who also fell captive while privateering under the American flag. Sadly, Ashburn would not survive his imprisonment, but Claypoole did, and after his release, Claypoole carried the unfortunate news of her husband's death back to Betsy.

Another year passed before John Claypoole married Betsy. Whether he had any reservations about becoming Betsy's third husband after her previous losses, we have no record. By all accounts, Betsy and John Claypoole lived happily together, raising their daughters and running their upholstery shop, located on 2nd Street above Dock Street before they moved it to Front Street.

Claypoole, however, continued to suffer from a wound he received at the battle of Germantown, and the last ten years of his life were spent as a semi-invalid cared for by Betsy.

> *While convalescing from a stroke, John Claypoole would share his dreams with his daughter which he thus described:*
> *"Why should we mortals vex ourselves with trouble, care and woe, When so much pleasure we can find walking to and fro?"*

After 34 years of marriage, Claypoole died. Betsy survived for another 20 years, lived with her daughters and never remarried.

Certainly Betsy Griscom Ross Ashburn Claypoole lived a long, eventful and productive life. In 1870, thirty-four years after her death, Betsy suddenly became an American icon — "Mother of the American Flag." Her grandson, in a speech to the Historical Society of Pennsylvania, revealed the long-held, but never before publicly shared, family story of the making of the first flag. Historians, to this day, continue to debate its credibility.

Questions also exist concerning the authenticity of the Betsy Ross House. The controversy over whether Betsy ever lived in that building cannot be put to rest, and many scholars doubt the claim. This debate originated in 1893, when Charles Weisgerber purchased the structure under the assumption Betsy had once lived and worked there.

Betsy Ross House circa 1895

Weisgerber's inspiration came from winning a $1000 prize from the city of Philadelphia for his painting of a historically significant event involving the city. Weisgerber came up with *Birth of Our Nation's Flag,* the now famous image of Betsy presenting the nation's first flag to George Washington. Spurred on by his success, Weisgerber mounted a fundraising effort to purchase and to preserve what he claimed served as Betsy's old shop.

But improprieties tarnished the effort when more than two-thirds of the money disappeared (purportedly into the pockets of the fundraisers, including Weisgerber). Much of the money came from schoolchildren who donated 10 cents in return for a certificate of thanks and a print of Weisgerber's painting.

When the Governor of Pennsylvania initiated an investigation, the foundation overseeing the project expelled Weisgerber from the board. Nonetheless, the irate and offended Weisgerber remained as curator of the house, and he lived there with his wife and family until his death in 1932. The scandal caused several newspapers to begin to question the validity of the Betsy Ross flag-making legend as well.

The Weisgerbers named the child they had while living in the Betsy Ross house Vexil Domus, which in Latin means "flag house."

With the controversy and uncertainties that plague the Betsy Ross legend and the Betsy Ross House, tales of the supernatural are not unexpected.

Several years ago at the Betsy Ross House, a visiting psychic claimed she saw the ghost of a sobbing Betsy at the foot of a bed in an upstairs room, implying that it might have served as Betsy's bedroom. Some believe that the few surviving relics from Betsy's time that still exist at the house, including furniture and personal items such as her eyeglasses, a quilted petticoat and bible, may act as a conduit for the manifestations.

Sobbing Betsy?

But, there may be a more macabre reason for the haunting based on the seldom-discussed dilemma concerning Betsy's grave. Her kin buried Betsy next to John Claypoole at the Free Quaker Burying Ground. Then, in 1857, their bodies were moved to Mt. Moriah Cemetery on the outskirts of Philadelphia. Approximately 120 years later, in preparation for the nation's Bicentennial celebration, Betsy and John were relocated once again, this time to the side yard of the Betsy Ross House.

Robbing a grave of its contents, even if only to transfer a corpse to a grander tomb... may call up the vengeful spirit of the person whose remains are disturbed. —Dictionary of Superstitions

However, one of the gravediggers involved in the re-interment reports that after digging six feet down they took what they could find and very likely left some of Betsy and John Claypoole behind. If true, the desecration of Betsy and John's grave presents a more plausible explanation for the haunting of the Betsy Ross House.

An obscure incident serves as the basis for yet another haunted tale at the Betsy Ross House. A bungled burglary led to the shooting of one of the perpetrators in the cellar of the Betsy Ross House. The incident created a sensation when investigators implicated a house security guard in the robbery, and subsequently charged him with murder of his co-conspirator. Ghostly whispers and disembodied voices emanating from the cellar's narrow hallways and low-ceilinged chambers are attributed to the double-crossed shooting victim.

Artifacts at the scene of the shooting

As with all hauntings, we can only surmise a reason for continued supernatural activity reported at the Betsy Ross House. Countless schoolchildren have learned the story of the birth of the American flag despite the controversy surrounding its origins. Questions of whether Betsy ever lived at that address still exist. Will the record ever be set straight concerning this legendary haunted house? Weisgerber, who spent much of his time and energy preserving the structure only to suffer scandal and shame, left strong emotional ties to the house. Shootings and murder are known to leave psychic imprints behind as well. And of course, disturbing the bones of the deceased conjures many a restless soul.

Final resting place?

From a letter dated 1945, courtesy of Betsy's ancestor, Lee Griscom, Ocean City, New Jersey, comes word of Betsy's supernatural powers:

It reads:

Daughter of Samuel & Rebecca James. This is taken from the family tree printed in 1865.

After the Declaration of Independence 1776, the 1st husband of Betsy Griscom, John Ross, had a cousin in Congress through his means Betsy Ross made the 1st flag authorized by Congress.

It is said she had the gift of healing which she exercised secretly for fear of gaining reputation of being a <u>witch</u>.

She had also a remarkable gift in foreseeing events.

Mad Anthony Wayne

Mad Anthony Wayne
Ghost Maker

Perhaps no man in American history can boast the number of connections to ghost stories and haunted locales as Mad Anthony Wayne. His fame comes from his ferocity and boldness in battle, and he proved one of the Revolution's most competent and effective leaders. Born just outside Philadelphia near what is now **Wayne, Pennsylvania**, Wayne left a legacy of daring deeds that are remembered in history books as well as in tales of the supernatural. Perhaps no other person carries a more befitting name than Mad Anthony Wayne, particularly concerning hauntings.

It seems that just about everywhere Wayne traveled, he left behind a ghost story. The most popular legend concerns the remains of his body following his untimely death at Erie, Pennsylvania in December of 1796.

The cause of Wayne's death remains uncertain. The attending physician characterized it as gout, although a modern-day diagnosis indicates appendicitis as a more likely affliction. Having died in the Erie Blockhouse, an American military outpost, Wayne was buried underneath the blockhouse flagpole.

Old Block House. A Monument in memory of General Anthony Wayne, known as "Mad Anthony", who died on this spot, December 15 th, 1796. Erie, Pa.

Thirteen years later, Wayne's son traveled to Erie to retrieve his father's remains for reburial back home. Surprisingly, Wayne's body remained almost perfectly preserved, which created a dilemma for his son, whose carriage could not accommodate the body. According to an article by Hugh T. Harrington, the attending doctor devised a rather macabre solution:

A large kettle was procured and as the body could not be boiled in one piece it was cut into convenient pieces and dropped into the boiling water. As the flesh separated from the bones it was carved away by Dr. Wallace and his assistants who scraped the bones clean.

The bones were then packed in a trunk. The water in the kettle, along with the flesh, knives and instruments used in the operation, were put back into the coffin in the original grave.

Following this grisly procedure, Wayne's son returned with his fathers bones and buried them at Old St. David's Church near the Wayne homestead.

The boiled remains, butchering tools and water from the process were dumped in Wayne's old coffin and re-interred at the Erie Blockhouse. Ever since, legend has it that Wayne's ghost rises from the grave on January 1st, the day of his birth, and travels the road between his home and Erie, primarily modern-day Route 322, in an eternal journey to unite his remains.

Site of Wayne's bones

Perhaps this became the defining moment in Wayne's supernatural legacy and the reason he appears in so many ghost stories.

Mary Vining, a Philadelphia socialite with whom Wayne had a long-time scandalous affair, became engaged to marry Wayne after his wife's death. On New Years Day, 1797, she received the devastating news of Wayne's passing. From that day to her death in 1827, she wore black and seldom left her house in Delaware. Today the Dupont building stands in place of her house, where, not unexpectedly, a ghostly lady in black lurks.

Mary Vining

Wayne broke yet another heart, a shattering that left behind supernatural residue as well. This oft-told story originated at Fort Ticonderoga where Wayne served as commandant. A local woman named Nancy Coates became Wayne's lover, but soon afterward drowned herself in nearby Lake Champlain after perceiving an unintentional snub by him in favor of another woman.

Nancy's ghost appears floating face up in the lake accompanied by the voice of a sobbing woman. Wayne's ghost also appears in the commandant's quarters, holding a mug and smoking a pipe.

Standing guard at Valley Forge

Horses play a big part in the spectral sightings of Mad Anthony Wayne as well. According to legend, the statue of Wayne on his horse in Valley Forge National Park periodically leaps from its mounting to dash across the grassy meadow. Another legend portrays the dashing duo at Chadd's Ford, Pennsylvania, where Wayne led his men in a maniacal raid against the British, allowing Washington to escape during the Battle of Brandywine. Horse and rider also appear at Storm King Mountain on the Hudson River in New York, where Wayne made a daring midnight ride to warn American troops of an impending attack.

Somewhere during Wayne's long line of military service, he experienced a kind of spiritual awakening — not unusual for someone who fought so many battles and survived against overwhelming odds time after time. Wayne tempted death and escaped its grasp to live and fight another day, and perhaps he began to wonder how long his luck would last. Maybe the curse placed upon him by a soldier he sentenced to death affected Wayne's outlook on his own mortality ... and affected his karma as well.

In 1792, while quartered at what is now Pittsburgh during the Ohio Indian wars, one of Wayne's men placed a curse upon him. Known as Trotter's Curse, the words of damnation were uttered against Wayne in what turned out to be a misunderstanding.

Wayne, in a drunken stupor, called for his orderly, John Trotter, who left camp to visit his nearby family for the day but without Wayne's permission. When informed of the missing aide, the outraged Wayne ordered Trotter's arrest and execution as a deserter. Taken into custody while walking back to camp, Trotter, in turn, became outraged at the unjust sentence and uttered an oath taken from the Bible against the men responsible for his death. It came from Psalm 109:

```
In return for my love they act as my
accuser … Thus they have repaid me evil
for good … And hatred for my love … May
[this curse] soak into his body like
water, like oil into his bones … May his
posterity be cut off … May his days be
few …
```

The men responsible for his execution reportedly died before their time, or suffered a series of illnesses as if the hex had taken effect. Even Wayne developed a sense of foreboding, ever anticipating misfortune. He lived only four more years.

This fear of the unknown affected Wayne in 1794 during the conflict with the Miami Nation in Ohio. Encamped at Fort Adam with his troops, a tree fell on Wayne's tent, crushing it before coming to rest on a stump. Although he suffered some bruises and cuts, the stump saved him from sure death. The near-miss had Wayne believing that instead of providential destiny saving him as it had in battle, the gods had finally turned against him.

> *"Issue the orders sir, and I will storm Hell itself"* - Wayne's response to Washington when ordered to attack the impregnable Stony Point fortress on the Hudson River.

A month later, when Wayne's men erected Fort Wayne on the sacred land of the defeated Miami Nation, his entire command seemed affected. Troublesome quarrels, desertions, court martials and drunkenness became daily occurrences for his usually well-behaved troops. Again Wayne attributed the mayhem to spiritual haunting — from their desecration of sacred land. Once he completed building the fort, he left, and never returned.

Wayne's name also appears in other ghost stories, even if his ghost does not. After three men were hanged in

York, Pennsylvania for plotting Wayne's assassination, their apparitions materialized at the site of the gallows in the town's center square. In Philadelphia, Wayne aided one of his soldiers in avoiding prosecution for the murder of a waiter — an incident implicated in the haunting of City Tavern.

St. David's Episcopal Church

Wayne's ghost reportedly appears in at least one other place — his gravesite at Old St. David's Church in Wayne, Pennsylvania. Some speculation exists that Wayne's appearance in the cemetery is somehow connected to his wife Polly. Although buried in the same graveyard, they spend eternity separated by row upon row of gravestones ... despite the availability of space at their respective sites.

We remember Mad Anthony Wayne as a man of indomitable will and spirit who became a legend in his own time. His legacy remains forever preserved in history books while he *lives on* in the annals of the supernatural ...

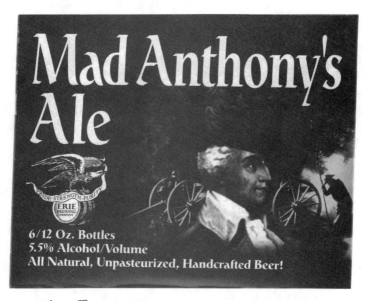

Erie Brewing Company perpetuates the legend
Circa 2007

Conjuring up the dead!

Revelations
Cults, Psychics & Miracles

Many of Philadelphia's ghost stories involve famous people or well-known landmarks. But the not-so-famous and somewhat obscure characters from the city's past have also left behind supernatural footprints. Three of those seldom-told stories of a surreal nature are featured here.

Jemima Wilkinson rose from the dead endowed with remarkable supernatural powers; Henry Seybert received instructions during a séance to make a gift to Philadelphia in honor of his mother; and Madame Blavatzky established communication with the "masters of the universe," leaving a legacy that exists to this day.

Despite their diverse backgrounds and outlooks on life, each left their mark on the City of Brotherly Love in their own fashion, of which a portion remains embedded in the ghostlore of Philadelphia.

JEMIMA WILKINSON

Jemima Wilkinson burst upon the Philadelphia religious scene and flamed-out rather quickly. As a disciple of universal love and universal peace, she called herself the "Universal Friend." Initially welcomed by the Free Quakers, Jemima's antics quickly led to her exile in New York State. Described as beautiful, vivacious and intelligent, she preached a polyglot of popular religious dogmas.

> " *She appeared beautifully erect, and tall for a woman ... every eye riveted upon her ... arched black eyebrows and fierce looking black eyes, darting here and there with penetrating glances ... as though she read the thoughts of people ... she spoke deliberately ... with a kind of croak, unearthly and sepulchral.*"
> —*Life and Times in Colonial Philadelphia*

But Jemima's most remarkable achievement occurred when, as a teenager, she rose from her coffin following her *death* due to illness. The near-death experience provided Jemima with extraordinary powers, including the ability to revive dead people, walk on water and see into the future. Her disciples even claimed to have witnessed her walk on the Schuylkill River by the falls above Philadelphia.

With the help of prosperous followers, mainly wealthy men, Jemima left Philadelphia and founded "New Jerusalem" in western New York. She enticed almost three hundred Philadelphia women to follow her to this promised-land where they renounced marriage and lived in celibacy. Reputedly, the men who did follow were relegated to work and kept separate from the women.

Jemima died in 1819 in her mansion in modern-day Penn Yan, New York, although her moral backsliding had resulted in her excommunication from the cult several years earlier.

HENRY SEYBERT

Scientists rarely support the precepts of paranormal phenomena due to their inability to empirically substantiate the claims of such phenomena. Nevertheless, countless supernatural events are documented around the world, many of which are not attributable to any of the disciplines of science. Perhaps this conundrum explains the actions of Henry Seybert, a wealthy scientist with a little-known Philadelphia legacy.

Henry willed $60,000 to the University of Pennsylvania for the endowment of the "Adam Seybert Chair of Moral and Intellectual Philosophy," which still exists today.

In the mid-19th century when Spiritualism gained worldwide attention as a blend of science, philosophy and religion culminating in communication with the dead, Henry Seybert abandoned his career as a scientist and devoted his money and energy to Spiritualism.

Henry never knew his mother, nee Maria Pepper, who died while giving birth to him in 1801 in Philadelphia. However, his father Adam, an eminent scientist who graduated from the University of Pennsylvania with a medical degree, devoted his life to raising his motherless son, bonding tightly with him into adulthood. Henry followed in his father's footsteps, attending college in Paris, becoming a member of the

Philosophical Society and establishing a world renowned reputation as a mineralogist, just like Adam.

But Henry's life changed at the age of 24 when his father died. He lost interest in his career as a scientist and instead pursued a transcendental interest that led him to Spiritualism. Henry's extreme emotional attachment to his father, manifesting as an obsessive attachment to his gravesite in Paris, France, apparently led Henry into the world of Spiritualism.

Henry never married, traveled extensively, spent considerable time in Paris and finally returned to Philadelphia for good in mid-life, first living at the southwest corner of 9th and Chestnut Streets before moving into a large house at 926 Walnut Street. His house became known as the Spiritualist Mansion, and he lived there until his death in 1883.

Henry's return heralded his complete immersion in Spiritualism. He had the bodies of his mother, sister and grandparents exhumed and reburied in Laurel Hill Cemetery where he could more easily visit with them. And Margaret Fox, the notorious medium from New

York State who, along with her sister, initiated the American spiritualism movement, moved into his mansion.

But Fox quickly became perturbed with the eccentric Henry, and returned to New York claiming Seybert "was in the grip of pure religious insanity" for expecting her to contact "nearly every saint, famous sage and ruler of old." Before Fox moved out, however, she held a séance in which Henry's deceased mother appeared with a message for her son. The long-dead mother Henry never knew, asked him to make a gift to the city of Philadelphia in her memory.

Today, that gift from Henry Seybert hangs in the bell tower of Independence Hall, a two and one-half ton copper alloy bell installed for the Centennial celebration of 1876 ... not as a token of patriotism from a wealthy citizen, but instead, to honor his mother, Maria Sarah Seybert.

Amid objections to the Seybert name being engraved on the bell, Henry changed the inscription to: "Presented to the city of Philadelphia July 4, 1876, for the belfry of Independence Hall, by a citizen."

Henry Seybert's gift hangs in
the Independence Hall bell tower

MADAME BLAVATZKY

The dynamic and captivating Madame Blavatzky took the spiritualist world by storm with her own gospel of universal consciousness.

Blavatzky came to the United States in the 1870s espousing a belief in "Masters of the Universe" to whom she could speak. They communicated via letters that had a tendency to fall from the sky at the most opportune times, usually when she wanted to convince people that her gods were real.

She nurtured an aura of mystery and divine knowledge, with tales of her travels to exotic locations including Egypt, Tibet and India, incorporating bits of their belief systems into her style of mysticism.

As with Jemima Wilkinson, Blavatzky's benefactors were people of means, although in the Madame's case she earned money and the allegiance of her disciples by communicating with their beloved deceased.

Her legacy includes the founding of the Theosophical Society, whose tenets include a belief in karma and reincarnation. A chapter of that organization still exists in center city Philadelphia.

Madame Blavatzky

On her arrival in Philadelphia in 1875, Blavatzky supported the burgeoning Spiritualism movement, and labored at establishing a noteworthy reputation for her mediumistic skills. However, Blavatzky became discouraged and outraged at the fraudulent mediums practicing in Philadelphia, and she abandoned the Spiritualists and formulated the ideas that evolved into Theosophy.

In the months Blavatzky spent in Philadelphia, she married a compatriot from Russia she hardly knew, from whom she soon after separated. She also became sick and languished on the brink of death before healing herself via supernatural means.

Blavatzky's medical miracle occurred in the townhouse where she lived on Sansom Street in modern-day University City. She fell and injured her leg, and when it became infected she ended up bedridden for several weeks. Unable to walk and reportedly near death, her doctors having given up, Blavatzky experienced a sudden inspiration of divine guidance. She placed her pet dog, a white dog, across her leg — the infection subsided in forty-eight hours.

> " *[her husband]* thought she was dead, her pulse and heart seeming to stop for hours . . . People say her spirit travels at such a time . . . "
> *Madame Blavatsky: Priestess of the Occult,*
> Gertrude Marvin Williams

The building where Blavatzky had this experience now houses the White Dog Café, at 3420 Sansom Street.

Carpenters' Hall circa 2007

Carpenters' Hall
Lingering Revenge

Lost among Philadelphia's favorite colonial attractions stands Carpenters' Hall where, in effect, our nation found its voice and destiny. Memorialized as the meeting place of the first Continental Congress, whose members included many of our founding fathers, it stands as testimony to the solidarity of the Revolutionaries. Those brave visionaries boldly created the Declaration of Rights and Grievances, stating in non-equivocal terms the Colony's intention to become independent of British rule. From those first secret meetings late in 1774, the framework for a new nation emerged and, as they say, "the rest is history."

Although just half a block from Independence Hall and the Liberty Bell, this almost forgotten artifact stoically lurks in the shadows of history in a quiet niche along Chestnut Street. Its ancient legacy includes some of the most respectable entities of early colonial times, and other *entities* not so well known or remembered.

Built in the 1770s by a guild of colonial carpenters, the building honors its centuries' worth of members with a prominent plaque near the entranceway.

> *Laying a hammer on the brow of a newly deceased person will facilitate the soul's flight to Heaven.*
> *- Ancient Folklore*

In addition to serving as a union hall of sorts for builders of that era, Carpenters' Hall also quartered many early Philadelphia organizations, including Benjamin Franklin's Library Company, the Philosophical Society, and importantly for our purposes, the Bank of Pennsylvania.

A notorious incident from the Bank's short tenure at Carpenters' Hall sparked a series of confused accusations, false imprisonments and rumors of murder. According to the legend documented in several publications, the taint of that affair still haunts Carpenters' Hall, and the story remains tightly woven in the fabric of Philadelphia folklore.

The Bank of Pennsylvania established operations on the first and second floors of Carpenters' Hall in the early 1790s when Philadelphia served as the nation's capital.

Controlled by Robert Morris, "the financier of the American Revolution," the bank played an important role in financing the growing economy of the new country.

In an era of few banks or financial institutions, bank robbery was an unknown crime. So, when in 1798, two men absconded with $162,821 from the vaults of the Bank, the deed instantly became the crime of the century for its boldness and for the audacity of its perpetrators. What followed were a series of misguided allegations and bizarre twists that played out over several months of an intriguing and bungled criminal investigation.

At the time of the robbery, Philadelphia suffered from an outbreak of yellow fever, and many people left the city for the countryside hoping to avoid the deadly disease. With substantially fewer people in town, the authorities were able to narrow the list of suspects to just a few likely candidates.

Shortly before the crime, new hardware and locking mechanisms were retrofitted on the iron vault doors located in the basement of Carpenters' Hall. With no obvious indication of forced entry, authorities immediately suspected an inside job, and the newly installed security system came under suspicion. The investigators quickly focused on the parties involved in the recent installation, leading them to arrest Isaac Davis and Thomas Cunningham, a security guard at the bank who also happened to live in a third floor room of Carpenters' Hall. Held in the Walnut Street Prison for a week, the suspects were released and, unaccountably, the charges dropped.

Apparently, Davis convinced the authorities that Patrick Lyon, the blacksmith contracted for the job, committed the crime. When the police discovered that Lyon had fled the city and could not be found, their suspicions, it appeared, were validated.

Indeed, Lyon abandoned Philadelphia, as thousands of others had in unusual haste, and headed for Lewes, Delaware. His companion and apprentice died shortly after arriving in Lewes, reportedly of yellow fever, the very reason Lyon would later claim that he had left the festering city to begin with.

As the headline-grabbing story of the bank robbery reached him in Lewes, Lyon calmly voiced his own suspicions that Isaac Davis, the man from the bank who hired him, seemed the most likely suspect. When informed by a friend that lawmen were looking for him, and only him, as the prime suspect, Lyon immediately returned to Philadelphia proclaiming his innocence.

From here on, facts and hearsay are somewhat hard to substantiate and separate, and the story veers into the world of the weird.

Upon arriving in Philadelphia, Lyon went to the authorities to proclaim his innocence and his suspicions linking Isaac Davis to the robbery. But the circumstantial evidence and previous testimony by Davis and Cunningham proved too convincing, and Lyon found himself sequestered in Walnut Street Prison charged with the crime.

Meanwhile, people around town were noticing Isaac Davis' frequent deposits of large sums of money at various banks, including the burglarized Bank of Pennsylvania. When authorities confronted Davis for the second time, he admitted to the robbery and agreed to return the stolen money.

According to Davis, himself a Carpenters' Company member, inside help came from Thomas Cunningham, who allowed him to enter the building, and then, using a duplicate key manufactured from Lyon's work, Davis and Cunningham looted the vault.

Davis returned the money and, in a strange twist of justice, left town a free man while, oddly enough, Patrick Lyon remained locked-up in prison, languishing in putrid, horrifying conditions, battling yellow fever with little food or medical care. Finally, after several months, charges against Lyon were dropped, and he left the Walnut Street Prison barely surviving the ordeal.

After his release from jail, Patrick Lyon wrote a book about his experience and then sued the bank for $12,000, a considerable amount of money in those days. He won the case and continued his career as a blacksmith. Isaac Davis was never heard from again.

Ironically, Thomas Cunningham, having contracted yellow fever during his short stint in jail, died of his affliction. And despite his trifling role, Cunningham paid for the crime with his life, while Davis, the mastermind, escaped without consequence. An injustice ... even among criminals.

Perhaps, as many believe, this was the start of the haunting of Carpenters' Hall.

Thomas Cunningham lived in one of the few small rooms on the third floor of Carpenters' Hall that at the time were made available to men who had no family in the area or no other options for housing.

The third floor as it looks today

Within a week of returning from jail, Cunningham died in that room, having contracted the dreaded yellow fever. Although death came rather quickly from the disease, the process of dying proved excruciating. Body fluids and blood leaked from every opening, including the eyes and ears, the stench overwhelming. As Thomas Cunningham quickly rotted to death, the awful smell permeated the building, and as much as heralding his demise, the disgusting stench seemed to proclaim his indignation toward his unsavory fate.

Shortly after Cunningham's death, the other tenants of Carpenters' Hall began hearing odd noises. They reported sounds coming from his old empty room and loud disruptive footsteps at all hours of the night ascending the stairway leading to the third floor, despite the absence of a person to blame. Apparently, the legend of Thomas Cunningham's ghost started immediately after his death, but it seems the sightings and supernatural activity infects the building to this day.

Revealed in the book *In Search of Ghosts* by Elizabeth Hoffman, the story of more recent hauntings at

Carpenters' Hall extends its paranormal legacy. In the 1960s, the O'Connors served as live-in caretakers, and they experienced several unexplainable encounters.

Stairwell to the 3rd floor

Noises from the abandoned third floor, heavy footsteps on the narrow steep staircase and an odd odor compelled the frightened caretakers to call the police. Of course the officers found nobody, although they did surmise that the smell emanated from a dead decaying animal trapped behind the wall. The police also informed the bewildered couple that they had investigated several similar claims from the previous caretakers, including calls to the fire company for unusual odors, but neither prowlers nor a source for the offending odor were ever found.

Evidently, the disruptions on the third floor continued throughout the O'Connors' tenure as caretakers, and there were reports of paranormal activity in other parts of the building as well, including the basement and their personal living space on the second floor.

In a 2005 interview, Tom M., a onetime gift shop employee at Carpenters' Hall, shared several unusual stories told to him by the O'Connors.

The most persistent sightings occurred on the second floor near the doorway that connected the living room and dining room. On multiple occasions over a period of years, Mr. O'Connor glimpsed a human-like form moving through the dining room while he sat in the living room. Mr. O'Connor never gained a clear view of the entity, but he described it as a featureless, vaguely familiar, ghostly being.

Mrs. O'Connor seemed to experience the greatest number of supernatural encounters while living at

Carpenters' Hall, including the unexplainable odors and phantom footsteps as well as a frightening encounter with an invisible entity in the basement.

Apparitions lurk in the doorway

Their son also encountered a menacing invisible presence in the basement during an overnight visit and refused to spend any time in the underground space.

Although Thomas Cunningham's spirit receives the blame for supernatural activity on the upper floors of

Carpenters' Hall, very little speculation exists on the entity that haunts in the basement.

Nevertheless, the basement did house the vaults of the Bank of Pennsylvania, making it the scene of the 18th century crime that led to Cunningham's ill-fated death. Perhaps, then, the double-crossed Cunningham also haunts the subterranean room in his eternal search for supernatural revenge.

Today, Carpenters' Hall stands as a member of Philadelphia's historically significant structures that played an important role in the building of a nation — a place where America's founding fathers came together to formulate a plan for a new country. But despite the many notable moments that are readily remembered, there are a few seldom-mentioned incidents that remain unforgotten as well.

Rappings, tappings, & footsteps from the Ghost Tour of Philadelphia!

I had a group behind Bishop White House and pointed out other significant buildings nearby: Merchant's Exchange, First Bank and Carpenters' Hall. One couple spoke up and said they had just visited Carpenters' Hall that afternoon and were forced to leave. I, of course, asked them why. They said that all of a sudden there was a terrible odor in the building. The fire department was called in and everyone was evacuated. The source of the odor was never located, and they said it was weird: all of a sudden they smelled it and just as quickly, it was gone. — Eileen's tour, 1999

Powel House

Powel House
Party On!

The stately home of Samuel Powel holds a few secrets, as one can only expect from a dwelling in which a prominent politician served his country in a time of turmoil. While the skeletons that may be hiding in Powel's closets remain there, the otherworldly visitors of his grand old home at 244 South 3rd Street freely lurk among its dark hallways and quiet rooms.

Samuel Powel's home, built in 1765, stands as one of the finest examples of townhouse Georgian architecture in America. His family lived there for over forty years, and it became a city landmark after a last minute reprieve from the wrecker's ball in the 1930s. Today the restored home operates under the guidance of the Philadelphia Society for the Preservation of Landmarks, which offers daily guided tours recounting the history of the home's colonial years while occupied by the Powels.

Samuel Powel, considered "one of the most refined Philadelphians of his time and one of its wealthiest," inherited an estimated 90 properties when his father died. Recognized as a deft and respectable politician, Powel served as Philadelphia's last mayor under British rule and its first mayor under the new United States republic.

Samuel Powel

Upon his marriage to Elizabeth Willing, progeny of one of the city's early accomplished families, Powel purchased the four-year-old house on 3rd Street where he and his wife established a reputation for lavish and gracious parties. The Powel's guest lists read like a Who's Who of colonial-era aristocrats, including George Washington, John Adams, Ben Franklin, the Marquis de Lafayette as well as Philadelphia's most powerful and influential citizens. The Powels were the center of the Philadelphia social scene even as the colonies began their secession from British rule and war erupted.

And among those many visitors to their home, according to several modern-day caretakers, it seems a few continue to survive from the 18th century ... as if the parties never ended.

Mr. and Mrs. Moore, who lived in the Powel house in the 1950s and 1960s, experienced several encounters with spectral entities, convincing them that perhaps the guests from long ago still frequented the old house — some of them quite well-known. In a 1965 article from the *Philadelphia Bulletin* they tell their story.

One morning as Mr. Moore began his descent of the front staircase, he saw the ghost-like figures of two soldiers coming up the steps toward him. According to Mr. Moore, "One wore a blue uniform. He looked up and smiled pleasantly. His teeth were very white. Suddenly he was gone." An acknowledged historian, Mr. Moore saw a strong resemblance between the smiling apparition and a frequent visitor of the Powels, the Marquis de Lafayette.

Marquis de Lafayette

Mrs. Moore's encounter with a famous historical figure, which she later connected to the traitor Benedict Arnold, occurred in the drawing room.

Late in the day as dusk settled in, Mrs. Moore entered the drawing room and, in the faint light of the evening, noticed a woman with her black hair pulled up in pearls, wearing a beige and lavender dress, sitting in a chair tapping her foot. In Mrs. Moore's own words, "She turned and looked directly at me. When I snapped on the light the chair where she had been was empty." Mrs. Moore was not as quick as her husband to put a name to the drawing room ghost, but a chilling coincidence several months later left no doubt in her mind as to the identity of the attractive woman.

Drawing Room

In preparation for an upcoming party, Mrs. Moore stopped in a local costume shop in search of a colonial-era gown to rent. She watched as the shopkeeper pulled out a dress known as the "Peggy Shippen gown." Mrs. Moore recounts, "It was the very same beige and lavender dress. I almost fainted."

The Moores experienced other, less dramatic phenomena while living there, and Mr. Moore attributed many of the unexplained noises to the normal creakiness of an old house: "... sometimes if you turn the light on suddenly [in the upstairs ballroom,] the whole floor squeaks as if a lot of people were moving about or you've interrupted some kind of [gathering]."

Lastly, the antique wardrobe in their upstairs bedroom unexplainably seemed to be the object of ghostly interest, its doors opening on their own regularly at four o'clock in the morning. If they locked the wardrobe, their bedroom door would creak loudly at about the same time, as if some unseen entity had established an early morning routine.

But the Moores were not the only ones with paranormal experiences at the Powel house. In interviews with several recent site managers and colleagues, additional unexplainable phenomena have surfaced as well.

From the Powel House archives, a 1993 interview of Cindy P. reveals unexplainable sightings in the building, once again on the staircase and in the drawing room.

Cindy recalls, "... all my experiences have happened either in the withdrawing room or right in the hall ... the first time I went into the Powel House, in the center hall at the top of the steps I saw a woman. I couldn't make out her face or anything like that, but she was all in lace, and behind her I saw a grandfather clock at the top of the steps." Unbeknownst to Cindy, at one time a grandfather clock did stand at the top of the steps, placing her vision at a much earlier period of time.

Cindy elaborated on the appearance of the apparition: "... the lace, it was like an ivory, like a bone color, it was not white, and I just got the feeling it was maybe handmade." She had other experiences as well: "... I've heard ladies outside the withdrawing room, I've heard them laughing, not laughing hysterically, but little chuckles and real quiet things like that."

Apparitions on the stairs

More recently, Del, a former site manager interviewed in 2005, shared his own strange experiences while living at the Powel House several years earlier. Again, the ballroom and staircase were mentioned.

Del awakened on several occasions in the middle of the night to the sound of footsteps, not just one set of footsteps, but what sounded like a dozen or more people milling about. The alarms never sounded, and despite a thorough search of the building, he never found anyone.

Del's daughter had her own close encounter as well. One day after they had just returned from the grocery store, Del noticed his daughter's startled reaction as she walked past the staircase. She explained that she had momentarily glimpsed, from the corner of her eye, the figure of a person on the stairs which just as quickly disappeared.

In yet another first-person account, the new site-manager Robert, also interviewed in 2005, experienced a different sort of phenomena. While walking through the section of the house open to the public, Robert saw a cat dart into another room. Thinking his cat had escaped from their apartment, he searched the room but in vain. When he returned to his apartment there sat his cat on his wife's lap. He told her about the cat in the other room, but she insisted theirs had not left the apartment. Still perplexed by his "ghostly cat," he mentioned the incident a few days later when he ran into the previous site manager, Mickey. She asked him what color markings the cat had, and he replied, "...black and white just like my cat." Mickey told him that her cat, also black and white, had died in the house while she was living there.

The prevailing theory attributes much of the paranormal activity, except the cat of course, to the period when the Powels so happily and successfully lived there. Many believe that Peggy Shippen may be the central figure in the haunting of the Powel House.

Stories of Peggy Shippen go beyond those we read in the history books, and fall into the category of legend. Some are unsubstantiated rumors or rationalizations to absolve or to blame her for the infamous Benedict Arnold betrayal during the American Revolution. The connection to the Powel House certainly falls into this category.

Peggy Shippen and Elizabeth Powel were related: Peggy's grandfather was Elizabeth's uncle. The Shippens were prominent members of Philadelphia society and were known to attend the festivities at the

Powel house. As Peggy matured into one of Philadelphia's leading belles of the period, she too would have attended festivities at the Powel House.

The politics and loyalties of the time were complicated, and although Samuel Powel served as mayor under the British, his sentiments were with the continentals, earning him the nickname of the "patriot mayor."

According to Shippen family genealogy, Peggy's great-grandfather Edward, was Philadelphia's first mayor, when Pennsylvania was governed by the Penn family in the early 1700s.

When the British army invaded Philadelphia in 1777, the British occupied many of the buildings in the city, including the Powel house. The Powels were allowed to stay, but they shared their home with a number of British officers. As they walked a very fine line of neutrality, the Powels continued to entertain, but with the British instead of the revolutionaries, as guests. Peggy Shippen attended these galas with British, and she became particularly enchanted with Major John Andre.

Andre and several other officers collaborated on a series of plays and other social events in which Peggy Shippen participated. Many of Philadelphia's young women were smitten by the handsome and talented Andre, although several sources link him romantically to Peggy Chew of Germantown.

The British retreated from Philadelphia after only nine months, and Benedict Arnold, appointed military commander of Philadelphia, led the returning American troops. According to Powel house history, Arnold fell under Peggy's spell while at a party honoring the returning patriots. Despite their disparity in age, Peggy only eighteen, Arnold thirty-eight, they married in less than a year's time. Many have wondered ever since if Peggy moved so quickly into marriage with Arnold as retribution to the fleeing Andre, who had left with the retreating British, or whether she had conceived a wicked plot to incite Andre's jealousy.

Historians postulate that despite her marriage to Benedict Arnold, an American General, Peggy Shippen continued to hold feelings for John Andre, a British officer. The depths and purpose of those feelings are still debated, and are inexorably linked to the treason of Benedict Arnold and his betrayal of the military fort at West Point.

John Andre   *Peggy Shippen*

Arnold's plan to turn West Point over to the British with Andre as the intermediary has caused speculation that Peggy, too, played a roll in the treasonous scandal.

Andre's capture behind American lines with plans for the treachery foiled the plot, and he dangled at the end of a hangman's noose for his part in the ruse. Meanwhile, upon hearing of Andre's capture, Peggy and Arnold fled to British controlled New York City. Eventually, the despised couple settled in England where they lived not only ostracized from their American roots, but distrusted by their new countrymen as well.

Some believe that Peggy's story is one of unrequited love, and she haunts the Powel house because of her time spent there with John Andre, her true love. Undoubtedly the center of attention and belle of the ball, she might have counted her days at the Powel house cavorting with Andre as the happiest and most carefree times of her life. In retrospect, whether a victim of circumstances or not, her actions led to a shattered life, forcing her to live in exile and shame, forever branded a traitor.

Reportedly, Peggy kept a lock of John Andre's hair until her death.

The otherworldly activity reported at the Powel House is associated with a number of rich and famous people of history. Some return perhaps to relive the good times of that long-ago period, others maybe to escape the fate of their mortal lives and to forget the secrets that led them awry.

Body Snatchers

When Dr. William Shippen began lecturing on anatomy in the late 1700s, he practiced his craft by dissecting bodies, usually those of unknown origin or suicides. Word spread quickly among neighborhood boys about the grisly goings-on at Shippen's place on 4th Street just north of Market Street. John Watson, fabled author of *Watson's Annals*, remembered the place still stood when he was a boy: "The lonely desolate house is still standing ... deemed the receptacle of dead bodies, where their flesh was boiled, and their bones burnt down for use of the faculty." The mysteries of the place led him to pen the nightmarish poem regarding his recollection:

> The body snatchers they have come
> And made a snatch at me;
> It's very hard them kind of men
> Won't let a body be!
> Don't go to weep upon my grave
> And think that there I be;
> They haven't left an atom there
> Of my anatomy!

The Bishop White House

Bishop White House
Divine Immunity

Feelings of sorrow and despair are not usually the characteristics one associates with a house, but the Bishop White House radiates such as if the emotions experienced there have contaminated its very walls, never able to be washed away. Perhaps a bit melodramatic, but nevertheless, many visitors attest to those overpowering feelings after touring the 220 year-old building.

In 1787, Bishop William White built the Federal style town-house located at 309 Walnut Street. White lived a long and productive life, serving as rector to Christ Church and St. Peters Church and leading the movement to organize the first American Protestant Episcopal Church. White also served as Chaplain to the Continental Congress and the United States Senate. Perhaps his best remembered deeds testify to his compassion for the sick and dying during the horrific outbreaks of yellow fever that decimated the Philadelphia population in 1793. Despite the Bishop's constant exposure to the diabolical killer, he survived the onslaught even as his family members perished.

> "... *Billy White was born a Bishop. I never could persuade him to play anything but church. He would tie his own or my apron around his neck, for a gown, and stand behind a low chair, which he called his pulpit: I, seated before him in a little bench, was the congregation; and he always preached to me about being good.*"
> — *Hannah Paschall, childhood playmate*

The Bishop's house now belongs to the Independence National Historic Park system, and guided tours are offered on a regular basis. Several buildings in the Park are known for their haunted history as well as their conventional history. But the Bishop White house carries the reputation among the park rangers as the "creepiest" building in all of Independence Park, and many avoid the house unless they are with someone. It seems the building is plagued with incidents that cannot easily be explained. The electric unexpectedly goes off, flashlights and cell phones go dead, their batteries drained, and visitors regularly report deep feelings of sorrow, a sense of pain and anguish, particularly while touring the kitchen area at the rear of the first floor.

What terrible things happened in that house to leave a lasting imprint of sadness after all these years?

The White family experienced their share of sad events during their long occupancy there. Just after moving in, they lost their youngest son, and a few years later the hellish yellow fever epidemic raged through Philadelphia, killing thousands in a horrible agonizing death. Many people left the city to escape the scourge, leaving behind deserted streets by day and the anguished wails and cries of the afflicted by night. The only signs of life were the death carts carrying the vanquished to the mass burial plots and the sick looking for someone, anyone, to relieve the pain and suffering.

Dr. Benjamin Rush, the preeminent physician in Philadelphia at the time, lived next door to Bishop White and worked long hours treating the afflicted. Undoubtedly the sick would seek out Dr. Rush, or perhaps even the Bishop himself, if their situation seemed hopeless. Certainly, the Bishop heard the doomed on the sidewalk outside his bedroom window suffering with their incurable disease, and surely he wondered how many of his congregation would survive the onslaught.

Although Bishop White's wife and youngest children fled to New Jersey, his mother, sister and two oldest sons stayed with him as the yellow fever plague ravaged the city. After his mother and sister succumbed to the diabolical affliction, he sent his sons to Trenton, New Jersey.

Despite the catastrophe, the Bishop stoically remained on duty while he sent his family to live in the uncontaminated New Jersey countryside.

Although informally ostracized by the public, as were all who regularly came in contact with plague victims, including doctors and ministers, he nevertheless survived the yellow devil, also know as "yellow jack," despite the thousands perishing around him.

Smaller outbreaks of the plague occurred almost every year in that last decade of the 18th century, and of course Bishop White could not escape the fear and emotional stress that affected the lives of those dear to him as well as of the members of his congregation.

On a more personal level, tragedy struck the White family again in 1797 when Bishop White's wife and another son were taken by dysentery. In the ten years in their house, the White's suffered through one calamity after another.

Bishop White's ability to survive the variety of plagues that descended upon Philadelphia during his lifetime while living next to the infectious Dock Creek has been attributed to his fondness for cigars and strong drink.

According to one park ranger interviewed in 1997, the unexpected deaths in the White family may provide the answer to unexpected sightings at Bishop White House. Over the years, several rangers have radioed reports of a shadowy figure moving about the kitchen and upstairs library. Their investigations have always turned up empty.

Some people believe the kitchen specter belongs to the White's longtime housekeeper, Mrs. Boggs. A psychic who toured the house in the 1990s gave a description of the specter that closely matched that of Mrs. Boggs. And according to those who specialize in the history of that period, her actions resulted in dire consequences for the White family.

The area around 3rd and Walnut Streets at that time contained many fine homes occupied by some of Philadelphia's finest citizens, including doctors, merchants and clergymen. About the only disagreeable feature within the immediate area was the notorious Dock Creek, which ran along the backyards of many of the homes. Outrageously polluted with putrefying human waste, animal entrails from a nearby slaughterhouse and every kind of decaying matter that today we route to sewer plants, the creek served as an open cesspool, harboring any number of diseases and disease carrying flies and mosquitoes.

However, for the White household, the more immediate danger existed in their basement.

The Bishop White house contained a special feature rarely found in homes of that period, an indoor bathroom. They located this "modern" amenity in the kitchen, an unfortunate location as it turns out. The waste from the toilet dropped into an open gully in the basement where, as needed, a bucket of water flushed the odorous waste along the gully and out the back of the White house into Dock Creek. But danger lurked in the dank and sultry cellar. The family's drinking water also came from the basement, where the well and sewer line were virtually side by side.

In an era when disease-causing microbes in drinking water remained undiscovered and the dangers of contaminated water were barely understood, this obvious "design" flaw in basic sanitation went unnoticed.

Unknowingly, the faithful and fearless Mrs. Boggs assumed the role of the "angel of death." She braved the yellow fever epidemic and remained with the Bishop through those horrible months of unrelenting terror. But Mrs. Boggs may have become the unwitting culprit in the deaths of the White family members who died of dysentery. Unbeknownst to her, each ladle of water she drew from the well possibly carried deadly germs, simply because of the well's proximity to the repository of human excrement ... an unsavory thought, but quite plausible.

Kitchen wing off back of house

Does Mrs. Boggs spend eternity blaming herself for the deaths of the family she served so loyally, and one would presume lovingly, for so many years? Could her never ending despair and strong emotional ties to the family cause the recurring manifestation in the kitchen, as witnesses to the sightings believe?

On a lighter note, an apparition spotted upstairs seems not to have a care in the world — oblivious to all distractions.

Serene and seemingly preoccupied in thought, the book-carrying phantom strolls contentedly between the library and the Bishop's former bedroom. Described as tall, slender and elderly with a crop of white hair, the specter resembles the Bishop in his latter years. He lived to the old age of eighty-eight, outliving all his immediate family and dying peacefully in the front bedroom in the company of his beloved relatives.

Bishop White

The turmoil and misfortune caused by the intangible killers of disease and pestilence haunted Bishop White throughout most of his life ... until he finally found peace at the end.

Physick House

Physick House
Is the Doctor in?

Steadfast and refined, the Physick House at 321 South Fourth Street bears the name of the "father of American surgery," Philip Syng Physick. Dr. Physick taught surgery at University of Pennsylvania, practiced at Pennsylvania Hospital, pioneered new surgery techniques and invented a number of surgical instruments. He believed in bleeding his patients to cure a range of ailments, and much of his learning came from experimentation on cadavers and autopsies. His legacy also includes heroic and unwavering service during the plagues of yellow fever that ravaged Philadelphia during the 1790s.

Today, the Philadelphia Society for the Preservation of Landmarks offers regularly scheduled tours of the building, and despite Physick's assured place in medical and Philadelphia history, his one-time home has an aura of mystery to it, caused, perhaps, by reports of unusual sightings within.

The beautifully restored Physick House stands today as a Society Hill landmark, just as it did when built in 1786 by Henry Hill, a wealthy merchant and wine importer. Hill earned a fortune importing Madeira wine from Portugal and spared no expense creating his 32-room town home. Prior to Hill's ownership, the sub-divided parcel encompassed a part of the city's almshouse, "an institution which contained an infirmary for the needy ill [and] special apartments for the insane..." Coincidentally, Hill perished in the yellow fever epidemic of 1798 before the house fell into the hands of Physick.

Philip Syng Physick

In 1815, Physick's spinster sister Abigail purchased the house and bestowed it upon her brother. Philip raised his children in the house and lived there until his death in 1837. In addition to performing surgery at the hospital and making house calls, Physick saw patients in his home as well.

Physick doctored many of the rich and famous of his time, including President Andrew Jackson, Chief Justice John Marshall and Dolly Madison.

Strangely, Physick's wife, Elizabeth, may never have lived in the house. Legend indicates that an argument over the removal of a tree on the property caused an irrevocable split in their marriage. Leaving her four children behind, she went to live in her father's house at 5th and Arch Streets where she remained for the most part bedridden.

Reportedly, she suffered from an undefined psychosis, perhaps manic-depression and possibly addiction to laudanum. Consequently, when Philip took the children to visit with her, he nervously paced the floor downstairs, refusing to see her. Elizabeth died relatively young, still in her 40s.

Elizabeth's father, Samuel Powel Emlen, was named after his cousin, Philadelphia mayor Samuel Powel. According to a modern day descendant, Emlen had a reputation as a mystic who possessed supernatural powers. Reportedly, people would cross the street when they saw him approaching to avoid falling under his spell.

Physick's ancestors lived in the house until well into the 20th century and at least one of those deserves mention. The last of Physick lineage to own the house, Elsie Wister Keith, suffered from what some would call eccentric notions. Oddly, she had an aversion to dust, whether connected to a medical condition or her own neurosis remains unknown. Her actions certainly seem unusual, however. Intent on eliminating as much dust-collecting surface as she could, Elsie remodeled the interior, and among other modifications replaced woodwork with ceramic tile and the original banister with a rounded oak railing. When she died in 1940, the house became the property of Pennsylvania Hospital.

Today, the Physick House, with many of its original touches restored, provides a step back to a time of genteel elegance. And, according to Physick House tour guides, on occasion an unexpected visitor appears.

The shadowy figure of a woman, described as wearing a long flowing gown and pausing here and there as if looking for something, appears unexpectedly within the house.

In 2003, several co-workers experienced their own close encounter with the ethereal being. While busily occupied with paperwork in a third floor office, a tremendous draft blew from the fireplace, scattering their papers onto the floor. Realizing that the sudden blast of air could not have originated in the fireplace (the flue had been sealed tight years before), they scrambled in fright into

COURTESY LIBRARY OF CONGRESS
Sealed fireplace in the Physick House

the hallway. But to their horror, a dark shadowy figure blocked their way. Then, as if in turn they had startled the phantom, it quickly moved down the hallway before disappearing into the wall. Call it "spirit intuition" or the power of suggestion, but all three were certain the apparition belonged to Mrs. Physick.

Speculation on the identity of the apparition haunting the Physick House has taken other forms as well. Perhaps the fastidious Elsie, with the dust phobia, returns periodically to check for her dirty nemesis. Or, as some believe, the lost soul roaming about dates back to when the "infirmary for the ill and insane" occupied the site. Another theory postulates that the spirit of one of Philip Physick's cadavers has taken up residence. For now, the enigmatic phantom still roams about making *house calls* at the old doctor's home.

PHYSICK HOUSE

321 SOUTH FOURTH STREET

OPEN TO VISITORS

Built in 1786 by Henry Hill, a prominent patriot and wine merchant, this Federal house is the last remaining of only three free-standing mansions built in this neighborhood in the eighteenth century. Hill imported most of the fine furnishings and fittings, including the fanlight which was said to be the largest one of any home in Pennsylvania at that time. In 1815, Dr. Philip Syng Physick, acquired the house. The interior restoration interprets the grand Neoclassic style fashionable in his day, and the collection includes medical artifacts that belonged to him.

This steel engraving of Philip Syng Physick M.D., was done in 1831 by Childs and Inman after a portrait by Henry Inman.

Dr. Physick saw patients at this house each afternoon between 2 and 3 pm. His patients included Dolley Madison, Andrew Jackson and John Marshall as well as persons from abroad. Renowned for his speed and dexterity, he performed surgery on the well-to-do in their own homes, a common practice before the concept of antiseptic surgery was understood. He also operated at Pennsylvania Hospital in the "dreaded oval room," the glass-domed surgical amphitheater which still exists.

Known today and in his own time as the "Father of American Surgery," Dr. Physick introduced techniques and designed instruments that were the vanguard of the practice of modern surgery.

Among his inventions still used are the stomach pump, catgut sutures and "rubber band" ligatures.

Dr. Physick lived at this address until his death in 1837. His descendants lived here until the mid-twentieth century, when the house became the property of Pennsylvania Hospital. In 1965, during the early years of the restoration of Society Hill, the property was bought and restored by Mr. and Mrs. Walter Annenberg, who deeded it to the Philadelphia Society for the Preservation of Landmarks to be opened to the public as a house museum.

This silver bain-marie urn belonged to Dr. Physick and is part of a larger tea service. The urn was made in Philadelphia by Chaudron and

The surgical tools above were used by Dr. Physick to remove portions of the skull. The contrivance to the right was designed by Dr. Physick to treat clubfoot.

A placard at the Physick House

Chestnut Street at 6th Street

Chestnut Street Phantoms
Family Curse

The busy intersection at 6th and Chestnut Streets hosts two of Philadelphia's most important historical monuments: Independence Hall and the Liberty Bell pavilion. Tourists from around the world congregate here, and as they stand contemplating the Liberty Bell, surrounded by its new glass enclosure, they might catch a glimpse of a beautiful young lady dressed in period clothes from the early 1800s. At first glance, she may resemble one of the colonial-era impersonators employed by a local tour company who wander Independence National Park. But if she appears agitated or distressed and suddenly vanishes from view, perhaps obscured by the bustling crowd in front of Independence Hall or by a clip-clopping horse carriage passing or by any of the other innumerable distractions on Chestnut Street — and she fails to reappear among the milling throngs — then perhaps the lovelorn maiden of Chestnut Street has materialized once again.

Opposite the Independence Hall complex on 6th Street looms the Public Ledger building. Before the rise of behemothian office buildings, homes and storefronts populated that block. People lived, worked and socialized in those old buildings and, over time, some were knocked down in the name of progress — others for reasons long forgotten. The residue of life from the generations that once lived there, however, may still exist.

6th & Chestnut Streets about 1800

In the early years of the 19th century, Judge Joseph Hemphill and his wife Margaret lived on Chestnut

Street near the corner of 6th Street. Under tragically similar circumstances, although separated by five years, two of Margaret's younger sisters committed suicide while visiting her from Lancaster. Many believe that reports of the ghostly maiden wandering nearby are the result of that emotionally disturbing time.

> *The soul of a person who commits suicide is condemned to roam the Earth forever.*
> *- Ancient folklore*

Research reveals a tangled tale of supernatural phenomena involving a wealthy Philadelphia family, a maligned United States President, a renowned poet, a preeminent china producer and an unorthodox antiques collector.

The saga begins with Robert Coleman, who came to Philadelphia from Ireland at age sixteen with the equivalent of just a few dollars in his pocket. Landing a job as a clerk to the owner of several iron-ore fields, he quickly established himself as a smart, reliable, opportunistic employee and found himself on the inside track of what in Colonial times equated to gold mines. Iron ore, the foundation of the burgeoning industrial age, lay in great quantities in the countryside around

Philadelphia. From this humble position, Coleman became the proprietor of vast acres of iron-ore, which he parlayed into great wealth to become one of the richest men in colonial America.

Robert Coleman's remarkable rise to prominence, a true rags-to-riches story, came with a price however, a horrible price. According to legend, a curse befell the family, leaving in its wake a haunted legacy spanning the hills of the southeastern Pennsylvania countryside all the way to Philadelphia's Chestnut Street.

In the iron-rich fields of Lancaster's Colebrook Furnace, a tyrannical mean-spirited ironmaster employed by Coleman, slaughtered a pack of acclaimed hunting dogs. Superbly told in the poem "The Legend of the Hounds," by George Boker, a founding member of Philadelphia's Union League, the story of pride, rage and betrayal portrays the anguished death of the maniacal ironmaster brought on by the return of the vengeful spectral pack of hunting dogs.

Shortly after the murderous debacle at Colebrook, a series of misfortunes descended upon the Coleman family, ravaging their wealth generation by generation until little remained. Their vast source of riches, the iron-ore fields of southeastern Pennsylvania, slowly slipped away, and the family suffered a plague of tragic events that took the youth and future of their dynasty.

> *Similar to the European Wild Hunt legend, Boker's spectral hounds still hunt on cold moonless November nights, their hellish baying portending ill-fortune for those who fall under their spell. The tale is still told at Halloween in the small towns dotting the Lancaster countryside.*

Sadly, the Colemans' relatives in Philadelphia could not escape the curse's consequences either. In 1819, Ann Coleman, Robert's 23-year-old daughter, reigned as the most desirable belle of Lancaster. Intelligent, pretty and from the richest family in Pennsylvania, she became engaged in August of that year to an up and coming lawyer, James Buchanan. Her parents disapproved of the young Buchanan, suspecting his motives leaned more toward fortune-hunting than romance. When Buchanan committed an innocent, yet unforgivable, social gaffe by visiting with another socially prominent and eligible woman during the course of business,

Ann's parents demanded she break the engagement ... which she did.

Buchanan's attempts to mend the rift and to explain the misunderstanding were repeatedly thwarted by Ann's parents. As the young couple's estrangement dragged on, Ann became depressed and disconsolate over the breakup.

In early December, hoping to raise Ann's spirits and maybe to introduce her to a new beau, her parents bundled up their pining daughter and sent her off to Philadelphia. Ann was joined by her younger sister Sarah, and the two belles from Lancaster stayed with their older sister Margaret, who owned a house on the 600 block of Chestnut Street with her husband, Judge Joseph Hemphill.

Directories from the 1820s put the Hemphill place at 144 Chestnut Street, which in those days was on the block west of Independence Hall.

Parties and social gatherings were in season as Christmas approached, but apparently, Ann remained broken-hearted over the breakup with Buchanan and uninterested in the festivities.

Shortly after midnight on December 9, having refused an invitation to the theater and having sequestered herself in her bedroom, Ann overdosed on laudanum, ending her young, unfulfilled life.

A first hand account of the sad and unfortunate incident comes from Judge Kittera of Philadelphia, a Coleman family acquaintance. Taken from his diary, it touches on the bewilderment and heartbreak connected to the loss of a young and promising life, with a prophetic reference to young Sarah.

"At noon yesterday I met this young lady on the street, in the vigour of health, and but a few hours after, her friends were mourning her death. She had been engaged to be married, and some unpleasant misunderstanding occurring, the match was broken off. This circumstance was preying on her mind. In the afternoon she was laboring under a fit of hysterics; in the evening she was so little indisposed that her sister visited the theatre. After night she was attacked with strong hysterical convulsions... her pulse gradually weakened until midnight, when she died… To a younger sister whose evening was spent in mirth and folly, what a lesson of wisdom does it teach. Beloved and admired by all who knew her, in the prime of life, with all the advantages of education, beauty, and wealth, in a moment she has been cut off."

Ann's death left permanent scars on the psyche of those dearest to her, including young Sarah. Unbelievingly, a similarly bizarre scenario would play out several years later with similar consequences.

In Philip Shriver Klein's biography on James Buchanan, the 15th American President, he quotes Buchanan's reaction when notified of Ann's death: "... I may sustain the shock of her death, but I feel happiness has fled from me forever."

Buchanan remained a bachelor his entire life and according to his secretary, when asked about marriage, he responded, "Marry he could not for his affections were buried in the grave."

Five years had passed since Ann's death, and Sarah, like her sister, fell in love with a man out of favor with her father.

Robert Coleman despised the assistant rector of their church, Augustus Muhlenberg, even as romance blossomed between Sarah and the young clergyman. A trivial dispute concerning evening services erupted into an ugly and personal vendetta spearheaded by Coleman. He forbade Sarah to have any contact with Muhlenberg as the dispute raged for over a year. Sarah remained faithful while the equally stubborn Muhlenberg refused to compromise his position.

Then, it seemed, Sarah's fortunes changed. Her father died from a lingering illness, and in a bittersweet moment, her obstacle to marriage disappeared. But the shrewd, old iron baron exerted his stubborn iron-will from the grave. Through legal stipulations in his will, he prevented any husband of Sarah's from sharing her inheritance.

In an eerie replay of her sister Ann's horrible fate, Sarah fled to the Hemphill's in Philadelphia, and like her sister five years earlier, Sarah ended her own life tragically and prematurely in Philadelphia.

With two suicides in a socially and politically prominent family coming so quickly one after the other under such similar and morbid circumstances, one can imagine the rampant whispers of early 19th century Philadelphians concerning the Hemphill place and the Coleman sisters. Were the Colemans cursed? Did the sisters haunt the Hemphill house? Were their disembodied spirits roaming the sidewalks of Chestnut Street?

Shortly thereafter, the Hemphills acquired Strawberry Mansion, the huge estate along the Schuylkill River then known as Summerville, distancing themselves from the Chestnut Street horror.

> After Ann's death, her aunt dedicated a poem to her memory from which the following stanzas come:
>
> Gone from the world, her gentle soul,
> Sudden and silent, winged its way,
> No hand could save, no skill control!
> God spake! And mortals must obey.
>
> Enraptured shade! Speed on, speed on
> Beaming with love and grace divine
> Approach the everlasting throne!
> Where seraphs dwell, where glories shine!

If the Coleman/Hemphill family saga ended with the deaths of Ann and Sarah, perhaps their story would have faded into obscurity long ago. But the well documented and much dissected story of the Coleman empire demise played out during the remainder of the 19th century, perpetuating the whispers of a cursed and doomed family.

Interestingly, the Coleman sisters' ordeal has taken on a supernatural connotation with the sightings of Ann's and Sarah's ghosts walking arm in arm with their forbidden lovers in Lancaster. Some people connect the sightings of female phantoms near 6th and Chestnut Streets in Philadelphia to the sisters as well.

As for the Hemphills, they became, at least temporarily, ensnared in a series of misfortunes, first the awful deaths of Margaret's sisters and then in a bad-luck business venture with a paranormal twist.

In the 1820s, William Tucker began producing high quality china in Philadelphia and developed a reputation for fine detailing and design. Nevertheless, Tucker struggled to make a success of the business, and in 1832 he convinced Judge Hemphill to invest in the china-works. Forming a partnership, they erected a new factory on Chestnut Street. Shortly thereafter, William, the driving force behind the enterprise, unexpectedly died, and within a few years the business failed. Judge Hemphill, trying unsuccessfully to salvage his investment, found himself with little but a forever shuttered factory.

Today, because of Tucker China's early American roots and relative scarcity, antique aficionados value it highly. Many pieces reside in museums, including the Philadelphia Museum of Art.

> One of the most prized pieces of Tucker china is "a rare hunting-scene pitcher with a raised decoration of horses, men and hounds on the body of the pitcher...," a scene eerily reminiscent of the Coleman curse.

Strangely, in 1997, nearly 160 years after the manufacture of the last piece of Tucker China, a bizarre book appeared on the scene, *The Psychometry of Tucker China: Philadelphia 1823-1838,* once again connecting the Hemphill name, and by extension the Coleman name, to the supernatural.

The author, Douglas Harkness, believed that Tucker china, many pieces of which were produced with no markings as to the manufacturer, could be divined through the psychic phenomena of psychometry. This methodology can be defined as a transfer of stored energy from an object to the person holding it, allowing the deciphering of information related to the object.

Harkness established an antique shop in upstate New York where, among other interests, he devoted his time to collecting Tucker China. He used the unorthodox method of psychometry to determine the authenticity of the china, relying on the powers of unnamed psychic mediums to identify a piece of Tucker China.

In 2002, after his death, Harkness' collection went to auction, attracting a number of serious collectors from around the country anticipating a once-in-a-lifetime opportunity to purchase the highly sought after china.

Disappointingly, as if long-ago investor Judge Hemphill, brother-in-law to the doomed Coleman sisters, had placed his own curse on Tucker legacy, only one piece of thousands proved authentic Tucker China.

> *"In the 21st century in... Mt. Morris, New York, where one man's prodigious lifetime collection of china and ceramics was being sold, there were no rappings or revelations."*
> —*Maine Antique Digest*

The curse that hounded the Colemans until almost nothing of a once great fortune remained left its mark on Philadelphia as well. Lost among the important historical events that transpired along Chestnut Street, their story nevertheless rivals any number of fascinating stories of the city's rich and famous, stories that chronicle the rise of a new nation, the ascension to great wealth and, in some cases, the fall to obscurity.

George Lippard and the Legend of the Liberty Bell

George Lippard, a popular mid-19th century novelist, is credited with creating the patriotic folklore of the Liberty Bell. The story, described as "that most thrilling and irrepressible tale of the bell, the vivid story of the old bellringer waiting to ring the bell on July 4, 1776," was widely imitated. It first appeared in 1847, in the *Philadelphia Saturday Courier* as part of the *Legends of the Revolution* series.

19th Century Philadelphia from Independence Hall

Ghost Town
The Restless Never Sleep

Of all the ghost towns in America, Philadelphia may be the most active, considering the number of ghosts who haunt the City of Brotherly Love. From the very beginning of European colonization almost 400 years ago and into the 21st century, ghost stories hold a special place in the folklore of Philadelphia, mesmerizing and haunting generation after generation.

Today, ghostlore enjoys a renaissance around the world, entering the mainstream consciousness with a constant flow of movies, television shows, radio broadcasts, internet sites, books, tours, ghost-hunting clubs and entertainment venues dedicated to the genre. As each new generation discovers the ghostlore of old, new connections and mysteries materialize. Philadelphia's contributions include some of the most famous hauntings of all, and following are a few more. Not as well-known as others perhaps, they are nevertheless just as titillating to the imagination...

ST. PETER'S CHURCH CEMETERY

Some believe that the existence of a portal to the *other side* explains the multitude of ghost sightings at the corner of 4th and Pine Streets where two ancient cemeteries coexist. Juxtaposed across 4th Street, St. Peter's Church Cemetery and the equally aged Old Pine Street Cemetery exude paranormal activity conjured up by the spirits of their restless inhabitants.

Of the two repositories for the dead, St. Peter's Church Cemetery ranks as the most active with ghost sightings recorded as early as the late 1800s. Several distinguished individuals claim the cemetery as their final resting place, including Commodore Stephen Decatur, a naval hero of the War of 1812; Nicholas Biddle, Philadelphia's own early

Decatur claimed to have seen the legendary Jersey Devil while test firing cannonballs in the New Jersey Pine Barrens.

banker baron; George Dallas, a former vice president for whom Dallas, Texas is named; Charles Willson Peale, the prolific colonial-era painter; and eight Native American Indian chiefs who died in the smallpox epidemic while visiting George Washington in Philadelphia in 1793.

Ghost sightings and supernatural encounters inside the tranquil looking graveyard continue to this day, leading to several theories for the weird goings-on. A former caretaker reported seeing the misty form of a female spirit with long flowing hair and gown walking among the tombstones in the south section of the cemetery before disappearing into the southernmost brick wall. A similar encounter occurred on the Ghost Tour of Philadelphia as told by tour guide Eileen:

My tour group was in the graveyard on the central walk facing southwest. A figure showed up on a customer's digital camera. I was in the picture and behind me was the misty form. You could clearly see the profile and long hair; below was just a white vapor. The apparition was heading south. Three couples fled out the back gate after viewing the picture and never rejoined the tour. The rest of us continued on — keeping a close watch on every picture taken with that camera! Revisiting the cemetery, I found that the tombstone where our unexpected visitor appeared belonged to "Fanny Gordon."

Another tale from a former caretaker involves a phantom cart *heard* on the central walkway. The sound of turning wheels and the clip-clop of a horse's hooves are distinct as it travels out the back gate.

Phantom death carts?

Sometimes the ghost of a black male accompanies the invisible procession, leading some to speculate that the manifestation has something to do with the yellow fever epidemics of the 18th century. Because African Americans were thought immune to the yellow fever plague, they operated the death carts that traveled from house to house collecting the dead for burial.

Finally, from an old-time legend comes the story of the ghosts of two Native Americans that would appear near the back wall of the cemetery. Reportedly, modern-day ancestors held a ceremony in the cemetery to help the wayward souls pass on to the spirit world.

PENNSYLVANIA HOSPITAL

The ancient relic of early American medicine lurking on Pine Street contains many fascinating and unusual tales — as one might expect of the first hospital in America. Some of those tales ooze into the realm of the supernatural, tainting a visit to the doctor with a certain level of uncertainty, so to speak.

The most renowned legend concerns the wanderings of an ethereal William Penn. According to an 1884 article by Elizabeth Robins in the *Philadelphia Press*, the Penn statue that once crowned the entranceway to the old institution would demount from its station to wander the grounds of the hospital. When one morning Penn's statue lay immobile at the door of the entranceway, residents claimed that he stumbled while stepping down, causing his rather embarrassing repose.

But less frequently talked about circumstances reveal startling tales of Philadelphia's own Quasimodo-like character and of a mad woman who haunts the old hospital's corridors.

Thomas Perrine, subjugated to the lunatic ward in the basement of the hospital in 1765, eschewed the relative comfort and security of those quarters for the cupola of the East Wing. His nails grew extraordinarily long as did his wildly-matted beard and hair, and for seven years until his death in 1774, he refused to leave the cupola. The sympathetic hospital personnel provided the one-time sailor with food and bedding, and despite the tiny space, Thomas survived the depravations of his solitary existence. Some people speculate that the spectral figure attributed to Penn's statue actually belongs to that old hermit Thomas Perrine, who now wanders the after-life where he would not go in life.

Reported sightings of a female apparition peering from a second floor window of the hospital allude to the sad tale of a woman gone mad. Stephen Girard, one of Philadelphia's most successful businessmen and greatest benefactors, had his deranged wife confined until her death in the lunatic ward of the hospital.

> *The Estate of Stephen Girard*
> The largest trust left to the City of Philadelphia is the one created by Stephen Girard. By his will, dated 1830, he bequeathed to the Commonwealth of Pennsylvania $300,000 and to the City of Philadelphia, cash and real estate amounting to over $6,000,000. – www.citytrusts.com

Stephen Girard arrived in Philadelphia in 1776 and amassed a fortune from shipping and commerce. He fell in love with and married charming Mary Lum, and the devoted couple lived happily together for eight years when, suddenly, Mary lost her mind. She became irrational and violent, and whispers of promiscuity were bandied about.

Despite his efforts to have Mary "cured," Girard deemed her situation hopeless, and, in 1786, Mary ended up in the lunatic asylum. Mary spent the last 25 years of her life confined in the hospital, her care paid for by Girard. Shortly after her banishment, Mary gave birth to a baby girl she named Mary. Sadly, the infant lived only five months. Much speculation exists that the child did not belong to Stephen, but the truth remains a mystery.

> ... *Mary was admitted as a lunatic ... after wandering through Philadelphia streets ... Girard [had her committed] ... Five months later she was pregnant and stories began to circulate that a black sailor got into the loosely guarded cells.*
> *—Life and Times in Colonial Philadelphia*

Shortly thereafter, Girard took a mistress, Sally, who lived with him for nine years before leaving to marry another man. Girard then took another mistress, this one twenty-six years younger than himself. Polly lived with him for 30 years until the last several years of his life. Girard died in 1831.

Mary died at the hospital in 1815, where she lies buried to this day in an unmarked grave at the corner of 8th and Pine Streets. Mary spent almost half her life tucked away in the lunatic asylum at Pennsylvania Hospital, never to leave, and upon her death, again tucked away in a corner not to be remembered. Perhaps Mary's restless spirit wishes to finally leave that hospital and regain her identity with a simple marker of where she spends eternity.

In 1979, Lanie Robertson wrote a play on Mary's confinement at Pennsylvania Hospital entitled "The Insanity of Mary Girard: A dream in one act"

REBECCA GRATZ

A rather non-descript building at 532 Spruce Street provides refuge for the ghost of a lovely young woman wearing a floor-length dress. Described as sad-looking, she keeps her head bowed to the floor as if in mourning. Memorialized in 1928 as the Rebecca Gratz Club, the building served as the Jewish Maternity Hospital and later as a half-way house for girls with emotional problems.

Today, apartments occupy the building, and Molly, one of the residents, shared her paranormal encounter in a 2002 interview. On several occasions Molly awoke in the middle of the night to the sight of a beautiful young specter standing at the foot of her bed, sadly gazing at the floor. Although she does not consider herself possessing any psychic ability, Molly nevertheless sensed a mother/child yearning during the experience, leading her to connect the phantom to the days of the old maternity hospital.

Former maternity hospital

But, some people speculate that the description of the young woman's spirit matches that of Rebecca Gratz, despite the fact that Rebecca died before the building existed. Rebecca did live close by, however, and is buried in Mikveh Israel Cemetery just a few blocks away on Spruce Street.

Rebecca established a reputation as a social reformer in the early 19th century for her contributions to the welfare of needy women in Philadelphia, as well as for an iron-willed devotion to her Jewish heritage. Her social service legacy includes significant roles in the Female Association for the Relief of Women and Children in Reduced Circumstances, the Philadelphia Orphan Asylum, the Female Hebrew Benevolent Society and several other charitable organizations. She moved in the highest social circles, and her accomplishments were well publicized and acknowledged.

In Ivanhoe by Sir Walter Scott, the noble and virtuous character of Rebecca of York is said to be based on Rebecca Gratz.

Curiously, Rebecca never married, which in those days constituted a breach of faith, as Jewish women were expected to marry and devote themselves to motherhood. Conversely, Rebecca fell in love with Samuel Ewing, a Christian, but her devotion to the tenets of her religion kept her from marrying him. Instead, she spent her life working to improve the plight of impoverished women while living with several of her unmarried brothers and sisters. When one of her married sisters died, Rebecca, characteristically, took her children in and helped care for them.

> *Rumors have connected Rebecca romantically to Washington Irving and Henry Clay as well as Samuel Ewing. Tellingly perhaps, upon Ewing's death, Rebecca reportedly visited his body and placed three white roses and a miniature likeness of herself on his heart.*

If Rebecca haunts somewhere in Philadelphia, one would suspect the home located on Chestnut Street she shared with her siblings for most of her life.

And the maternity ward on Spruce Street built in Rebecca's honor? As with most places associated with life and death, an abundance of ghost sightings may not be unusual — even if their ethereal identities remain elusive.

THE BOURSE

Situated along Independence Mall on 5th Street between Market and Chestnut stands a relic from America's Gilded Age, a period of great economic growth at the end of the 19th century. Finished in 1893 under the direction of George Bartol, the Bourse served as a merchant exchange, housed the first American commodities exchange and functioned for decades as the center of Philadelphia's commerce and trade.

New owners took over the building in 1979 and remodeled its nine stories. They installed food and retail shops on the first floor and business offices above.

Not surprisingly, the renovations disturbed some forgotten tenants who, having laid claim to that plot years earlier, were now disrupted. In 2004, a retired electrical union worker shared his tale of phantoms at the Bourse and spooked workers: "We were refurbishing the inside, and one really cold winter morning as I was starting the portable heaters, one of our guys comes walking towards me with a look of fear on his face. I asked what was wrong, and he swore he had just seen two soldiers dressed in uniform —

Revolutionary soldiers, kind of fuzzy, just standing there staring at him. He was really shaken up and wouldn't go back inside."

Despite its well-known mercantile history, another not so well-known institution once occupied the site of the Bourse. For nearly a hundred years beginning in the early 1700s, the Sparks Burial Ground of Seventh-Day Baptists served as the final resting place for its parishioners. In the name of progress, as the city's business district expanded, the corpses were dug out and removed. Reputedly, the gravediggers missed a few occupants, and they remain entombed underneath the sidewalk along 5th Street, perhaps explaining the phantom soldiers of the Bourse.

WASHINGTON SQUARE

Tranquil and inviting, Washington Square provides an oasis of pastoral pleasure amid the helter-skelter city scene. But concealed underneath its shaded walkways and verdant lawn, lie the bodies of thousands of people buried here centuries ago when the park served as a potter's field.

Washington Square shares the Walnut and Sixth Street corner with Independence Square, and dates to the original layout of the city as designed by William Penn — one of five squares to serve as public parks. Almost from the beginning, however, Washington Square served as the city's potter's field, where the poor and outcasts of society were buried.

Joshua Carpenter's daughter, buried in the center of the square, became the first recorded burial after committing suicide in the early 1700s. Speculation points to that ignominious event as placing a curse on Washington Square, resulting in centuries of ghost sightings at the park.

From the annals of Philadelphia folklore comes the most famous and often-told ghost story of Washington Square. An elderly Quaker woman took it upon herself to act as a guardian of the dead. She regularly patrolled the square, even sleeping between the long-ago markers to prevent grave robbers from digging out the bodies. When she died, her ghost continued her earthbound duty, keeping eternal vigilance over the dead bodies.

But stories of supernatural activity in Washington Square continue to this day, and here are a few collected from the Ghost Tour of Philadelphia.

According to long-time tour guide Nick, a woman, having recently recovered from an auto accident and visiting from Ohio, experienced a strange vision at Washington Square:

They were walking towards Washington Square Park on Locust Street, and almost the minute the park was in her view the woman stopped. At first her friends didn't notice because they were caught up in conversation. It was when they went to say something to her that they realized she was several feet behind them just staring into the park. It seemed as if she was mumbling to herself. As they got closer they heard her saying, "What are they doing there? Why are they just standing around like that, why don't they go!" She refused to take even one step closer to the park, and in fact they had to go several blocks out of their way to make sure she couldn't even see it. Later on, after she calmed down, they asked her what she had seen. With some hesitation, she admitted that since the accident she believed one of two things was happening to her. Either she was going insane or she could see ghosts. She wasn't positive which one it was until she saw that park. She said dozens of "people" were just wandering around inside its walls as if they were trapped there. She had never seen so many ghosts in one place just doing nothing like that . . . nothing but watching the living.

From Michelle, another long-time tour guide, comes this intriguing tale:
I had a tour group from somewhere in the Midwest. A number of the kids wanted to tell me their own personal ghost stories from back home. So we're walking and talking and finally this little girl, about eight, comes up to me and says, "My sister sees ghosts."

Then the little sister starts telling these creepy little stories her sister had told her. One was about their dead grandmother, who visited them in their room at night. Another was about their [dead cat] she hears meowing at the foot of their bed.

By the time the younger sister told me her last tale, we're entering Washington Square. At this point, I have other kids telling me different stories, but I notice that the girl who sees ghosts is staring off at the southwest corner of the Square. Finally, she turns to me and asks, "Did you see that girl back there?" I look at the corner and see nothing. She continues, "You didn't see a girl back there? The one with the hat and the dress?" Then she described a young woman dressed as a Quaker would have been in the colonial era. Considering the detail on the hat and dress, and the number of people buried inside Washington Square, I thought perhaps she'd had a glimpse of someone buried there long-ago.

SHIPPEN WAY INN

In the section of town once known as Southwark, on a street once called Shippen Lane, stands the quaint bed and breakfast Shippen Way Inn. Named after the city's first mayor, Edward Shippen, part of the structure dates back to the mid 1700s when it served as housing for dock workers.

The current owner purchased two row homes, 416 and 418 on Bainbridge Street, from a man he called Bow Wow Bowser, and connected them to create the nine-room inn.

Bow Wow had lived in 416 and had purchased 418 for his son as a wedding gift, although that property had no plumbing or modern amenities. Bow Wow had an infamous past, having escaped from Eastern State Penitentiary with the considerably more infamous bank robber Wee Willie Sutton. Bow Wow also claimed he shot a woman outside his home on Bainbridge Street.

In a 2003 interview, the current innkeeper shared the tale of a haunted room at the inn — the dormer room where Bow Wow's daughter-in-law reportedly committed suicide by hanging.

Since the conversion to an inn, several guests claim to have been disturbed by the sound of disembodied footsteps in the dormer room. The innkeeper also confirmed that he experienced the unexplainable footsteps while alone in that room.

Does the spirit of the beleaguered daughter-in-law who committed suicide in her wedding-gift-house haunt the dormer room? It seems likely!

DEBORAH LOGAN

One of Philadelphia's more obscure historical sites lingers in the far northern Germantown section of the city. Built in the 1720s by James Logan, this ancient structure, named Stenton, dates back to the early days of the Pennsylvania colony. Located at 4601 North 18th

Street, the restored estate offers regular tours under the direction of The National Society of the Colonial Dames of America.

Stenton

James Logan accompanied William Penn on his voyage to the colony in 1699 and became the primary administrator and agent for the Penn family. A prominent Quaker and businessman, Logan also served as governor of Pennsylvania.

Stenton's brush with the supernatural comes from Deborah Logan, wife of James' grandson George, when they resided at Stenton in the 19th century. Born Deborah Norris, she lived near Independence Hall and attended the first reading of the Declaration of Independence as a 15-year-old girl. As an adult, she became an accomplished historian and writer, recognized by her election as the first female member of the Historical Society of Pennsylvania.

Some of Deborah's most important work included the transcription of James Logan's papers that chronicled the early history of Pennsylvania. That effort brought forth an extraordinary tale of her encounter with the ghost of James Logan as told in the book *Penn's Green Country Towne.*

While writing an account of her husband's famous grandfather, Deborah became engrossed in the task to the point she dreamt of the work at hand ...

She had been for a day or two toiling over a letter from Logan to Penn, on which the mice and the mould had been contending for generations and where 'it was hard to name the victors.'

One morning, while struggling with the transcription, she gazed at the portrait of James Logan hanging on the wall and spoke to it:

Honored ancestor of my worthy husband, I deeply wish that thou couldst unravel my riddle!

To her wonder, the eyes in the portrait moved and the mouth parted and replied:

Dear child of my house, I thank thee for the great care which thou hast taken to preserve the memory of my governor, William Penn, and that of my less worthy self … I was born in Ireland of a Scotch family. My wife Sarah Reed was ever a true helpmeet to me. I ever tried to perform the business of William and Hannah Penn most faithfully, and they treated me as a brother. I was for a time the President of the young Province.

Talking portrait

For forty years I served Penn … I loved
the dear Indians, and they loved me …

I labored to lead a Christian life … My
worthy granddaughter, so spend thy
earthly years that the eternal years at
God's right hand … may be thy lot.

Her wish fulfilled, the portrait returned to its normal
countenance, and Deborah completed her work. She
contentedly spends eternity "buried in an old graveyard
near the mansion."

GEORGE WASHINGTON

The metaphysical tales of George Washington's life
serve many purposes whether allegorical or
inspirational. One with a decidedly supernatural bent
portrays a vision visited upon Washington by an angel
while encamped just a short distance from Philadelphia
at Valley Forge in the winter of 1777 — a prophecy of the
trials and tribulations for the newborn United States of
America.

The story, recorded by Wesley Bradshaw in 1859, came
to light in an interview with Andrew Sherman, aged 99,
whom Bradshaw met while attending Fourth of July

festivities at Independence Square in Philadelphia. Sherman's first-hand account begins:

```
[Washington] remained in his quarters
nearly all the afternoon alone. When he
came out, I noticed that his face was a
shade paler than usual … with that
strange look of dignity which he alone
commanded, related the event that
occurred that day.
```

There follows a lengthy description of Washington's encounter with an ethereal figure that prophecies three major conflicts with America emerging triumphant in all. Interpretations identify the conflicts as the Revolution, the Civil War, and World War I or II or Armageddon. The missive resides in the Library of Congress. Following are key excerpts:

```
… as I was sitting at this table engaged
in preparing a dispatch, something seemed
to disturb me. Looking up, I beheld
standing opposite me a singularly
beautiful female … A new influence,
mysterious, potent, irresistible, took
possession of me. All I could do was to
gaze steadily, vacantly at my unknown
visitor … the mysterious visitor herself
becoming more airy, and yet more distinct
to my sight than before.
```

Presently I heard a voice saying, 'Son of the Republic, look and learn' … I now beheld a heavy white vapor at some distance rising fold upon fold … Before me lay spread out in one vast plain all the countries of the world …

… I beheld a dark, shadowy being, like an angel floating in mid-air, between Europe and America … Immediately a dark cloud raised from these countries and joined in mid-ocean … it enveloped America in its murky folds. Sharp flashes of lightning passed through it at intervals, and I heard the smothered groans and cries of the American people.

… The dark cloud was then drawn back to the ocean … villages and towns and cities springing up one after another until the whole land from the Atlantic to the Pacific was dotted with them.

Again I heard the mysterious voice say, 'Son of the Republic, the end of the century cometh, look and learn.'

At this the dark, shadowy angel turned his face southward, and from Africa I saw an ill-omened spectre approach our land. It flitted slowly over every town and city. The inhabitants … set themselves in battle array against each other … a bright angel … bearing the American flag, which he placed between the divided nation … said, 'Remember ye are brethren.' Instantly the inhabitants … became friends once more…

And again I heard the mysterious voice saying, 'Son of the Republic, look and learn.' At this the dark, shadowy angel placed a trumpet to his mouth and blew three distinct blasts … there gleamed a dark red light by which I saw … vast armies devastate the whole country and burn the villages, towns, and cities … the dark, shadowy angel placed his trumpet once more to his mouth and blew a long and fearful blast.

Instantly a light as of a thousand suns shone down from above … At the same moment the angel … who bore our national flag in one hand and a sword in the other, descended from the heavens, attended by legions of white spirits … Instantly the dark cloud rolled back, together with the armies it had brought, leaving the inhabitants of the land victorious.

… I found myself once more gazing upon the mysterious visitor, who, in the same voice I had heard before, said, 'Three great perils will come upon the Republic …' With these words the vision vanished, and I started from my seat, and felt that I had seen a vision wherein had been shown me the birth, progress, and destiny of the United States.

There exists another prophecy with a supernatural twist concerning Washington. In 1755, during the French and Indian War, Washington and his troops were badly outnumbered. Washington sat tall on his horse, an easy target for the Indians as he tried to rally his men. Afterwards, he wrote his brother, "I had four bullets through my coat, two horses shot [from] under me, yet escaped unhurt …," In 1770, Washington met an Indian chief who had participated in the battle and who prophesied that Washington would become the leader of a great nation. His reasoning being that during the battle, he and many of his men took deliberated aim on the exposed Washington, but it was as if an invisible force deflected the bullets, leaving the chief to conclude that Washington was protected by the Great Spirit.

BEN FRANKLIN

Ben Franklin's legacy haunts just about every civic institution in Philadelphia, from the library to the hospital to the fire department to the university, and on and on. Indisputably a man of the ages, Ben's propensity for doing good for the community and his fellow man helped shape and define, not only Philadelphia, but the United States of America as well.

When it comes to Ben's ghost, sightings are as prolific as his accomplishments. Among his otherworldly hangouts are Library Hall, Franklin Court, Powel House and Pine Street Cemetery. Or, you might catch him hovering about his grave late at night gathering the pennies with which tourists shower his grave all day long. For as Ben would say: *a penny saved is a penny earned,* and *if riches are yours ... take them with you to the other World*!

Ben became famous for his contributions to society, many of which benefited Philadelphia directly. Through his alter ego, Richard Saunders, and the publishing of *Poor Richard's Almanac*, Ben began his assent to the worthy citizen people admire, while abiding by a Poor

Richard adage of: *If you would not be forgotten as soon as you are dead and rotten, either write things worth reading or do things worth writing.*

Benjamin Franklin's Tomb

Among Ben's many interests, was of course, life after death, and he expressed his optimism of the here and after in: *Fear not death, for the sooner we die, the longer shall we be immortal!*

He lived up to his reputation as a pragmatist, however, by making a pact with his best friend, that "the one who happened first to die should ... make a friendly visit to the other." Ben survived his friend, but never heard from him again.

Franklin also published the *Pennsylvania Gazette*, in which he wrote a ghost story he called "Letter of the Drum":

I know well that the Age in which we live, abounds in … *Free-Thinkers*, … and treat the *most sacred Truths* with Ridicule and *Contempt*: … not only deny the *Existence* of the *Devil*, and of *Spirits* in general, but would also persuade the World, that the Story of *Saul* and the *Witch of Endor* is an Imposture; and which is still worse, that no Credit is to be given to the so well-attested One of the *Drummer* of *Tedsworth*.

I do, indeed, confess that the Arguments of some of these unbelieving Gentlemen, with whom I have heretofore conversed on the Subject of *Spirits*, Apparitions, *Witches*, &c. carried with them a great Shew of Reason, and were so specious, that I was strongly inclined to think them in the Right; and for several Years past have lived without any Fear or Apprehensions of *Daemons* or *Hobgoblins*; but the Case is quite alter'd with me now; and I who used to sleep without drawing my Curtains, am now so fearful, that I pin them every Night I go to Bed with corking Pins, and cover my self Head over Ears with the Clothes.

Now this Change is not owing, as you would imagine, to any frightful Apparition I have seen, or uncommon Noise I have heard; but to a most amazing Account I received the other Day from a Reverend Gentleman, of a certain House's being haunted with the *D* ------ *l* of a Drummer, not a whit less obstreperous, than the *Tedsworthian* Tympanist:

This Gentleman, whose Veracity few People presume to call in Question, told me, that he was not long since obliged to meet some of his Brethren, at a certain Town about fifteen Miles below Philadelphia, … they spent the Evening chearfully, yet soberly; that about ten at Night they retired to repose themselves, but lodged in separate Rooms; that he, with his Companion, were no sooner warm in their Bed, than they heard a Drum beating very loud, now on the one Side of their Bed, then on the other, … that the Noise continued all Night, frighted them almost to Death, and yet, which is the most surprizing and unaccountable Part of the Relation, disturbed no Mortal in the House save themselves;

… early in the Morning they went into the next Room, where they found two of their Brethren sleeping soundly; that they were amazed to find them so fast asleep after such a terrible Night; that having

awakened them, they asked whether they
had not been disturbed with the Noise of
a Drum? that they replied, They had
rested well, and were surprized to hear
them ask such a Question, and hinted that
they believed them to be out of their
Senses; upon which he related to them the
Adventure of the Night, so full of
Horror, with all the Particulars I have
mentioned, and many more which I have
omitted;

That at first they seemed to give little
Credit to what he said; but upon his
Bedfellow's affirming it to be true, they
appeared to be satisfied of the Reality
of the Fact.

Then the Gentleman went on with his Story
in this wise: That the next Night he with
his Companion went to Bed in the same
Room, in which they had been so terribly
frighten'd; that they had not taken their
first Nap, before they heard an uncouth
Noise under them; that his Companion was
shortly after seized violently and
forcibly by the great Toe, and in great
Danger of being pulled out of the Bed;
but that upon the Beating of the Drum,
which happen'd at the same Instant, his
Toe was released; and that to prevent any
future Attacks, they hoisted their Knees
up to their very Noses;

… the Noise still growing louder, they felt a most prodigious Weight on them, heavier, as he said, than the *Night-Mare*; that by his Voice they presently discovered it to be one of their Brethren, who had come into their Room on purpose to scare them; either believing that they had told him a Fib, or that they were under such potent Influences the Night before, as made them imagine they heard a Drum, when in Reality they did not;

But mark, said the Relater to me; according to the old Proverb, *Harm watch Harm catch*; for he was so frighted himself, that he would not have ventured back to his own Room, though he were sure to be made a Bishop; so that we were obliged to share our Bed with him, in which we lay sweating, and almost dead with Fear, 'till Morning.

Thus he concluded his surprizing Relation, which wrought so strongly on me, that I could no longer Doubt of the D ------ l's having plaid them this Prank; and to this Story only my Timorousness is owing.

WILLIAM PENN

William Penn's legacy transcends that of most other British colonists in America, perhaps because, from the very beginning, his purpose centered on metaphysical beliefs. Intent on establishing a place for freedom of worship, regardless of denomination, Penn's "Holy Experiment" morphed from the religious haven of Penn's Woods and Philadelphia, the City of Brotherly Love, into the keystone of independence from British rule, leading eventually to a new nation — the United States of America.

This rhetorical summary of 100 years of history had its start with William Penn, who experienced a spiritual awakening through a miraculous vision at the age of eleven or twelve.

Deemed a "visitation of heavenly light," the episode occurred while Penn sat alone in his room at boarding school. Suddenly overcome with a feeling of happiness, Penn's room filled with a soft glowing light characterized as a manifestation or psychic vision. This encounter convinced him of the existence of a God, and it set out his life's path, leading him to the Quaker religion and the founding of Pennsylvania.

William Penn

Penn's tolerance of an individual's metaphysics can perhaps best be characterized by the following anecdote:

In the late seventeenth century, witches were still feared and persecuted by some people. Even Quakers were occasionally accused of partaking in their wickedness.

One such elderly woman, put on trial for witchcraft, came before William Penn for judgment.

"Art thou a witch?" he asked her. "Hast thou ever ridden through the air on a broomstick?" The accused showed no remorse and admitted to such.

Penn told her, in effect, that he knew of no law against it and recommended that the jury dismiss her. So they found her guilty not of witchcraft, but merely of having the "common fame of being a witch" and set her free.

From the very beginning Penn's colony accepted those of varying beliefs and cultures, a hodgepodge of people melded into a new society, tolerant not only of freethinkers, but eccentrics as well.

THE REPEAL. — or the Funeral Procession. of MISS AMERIC-STAMP.

Early American political cartoon on death and taxes

As Philadelphians continue to make history for the history books, their odd, peculiar tales of the unknown will lie entombed between those lines of history — the seldom told tales of ghosts, haunted houses and spirits that lurk in the dark!

But like the Philadelphians who came before them, those strange and unbelievable tales of the unknown will continue to haunt the *quick and the dead*!

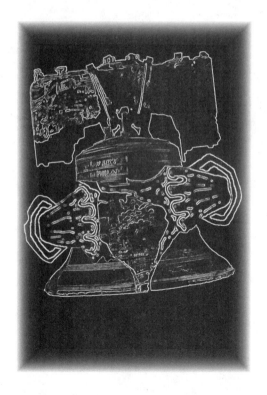

Ghost Stories of Philadelphia, PA

Acknowledgements

Editor: Alanna Lynne Reeser

Boker, George. *"The Legend of the Hounds"*
Burr Agnes Rush. *Russell H. Conwell and His Work: One Man's Interpretation of Life*
Cotter, John L., Roberts, Daniel G., Parrington, Michael. *The Buried Past*
Crawford, Mary Caroline. *Romantic Days in the Early Republic*
Earle, Alice Morse. *Two Centuries of Costume in America*
Etting, Frank Marx. *The Old State House of Pennsylvania*
Franklin, Benjamin. *The Autobiography of Benjamin Franklin*
Guiley, RoseMary Ellen. *The Encyclopedia of Ghosts and Spirits*
Harker, John Balderston. *Betsy Ross's Five Pointed Star*
Harland, Marion. *More Colonial Homesteads and Their Stories*
Hotchkin, Rev. S. F. *Penne's Greene Country Towne*
Keels, Thomas H. *Philadelphia Graveyards and Cemeteries*
Kelley, Jr., Joseph J. *Life and Times in Colonial Philadelphia*
Lombroso, Cesare. *After Death What?*
Marion, John Francis. *Bicentennial City*
Miller, E. Willard. *Pennsylvania, Keystone to Progress, An Illustrated History*
Mitchell, Edwin Valentine. *It's an Old Pennsylvania Custom*
Oberholtzer, Ellis Paxson. *The Literary History of Philadelphia*
Penn Mutual Life Insurance Company. *The Independence Square Neighborhood*
Pickering, David. *Dictionary of Superstitions*
Powell, J. M. *Bring Out Your Dead*
Raisin, Max. *A History of the Jews in Modern Times*
Scharf, John Thomas and Westcott, Thompson. *History of Philadelphia 1609-1884*
Spears, John R. *Anthony Wayne: Sometimes Called "Mad Anthony"*
Ukers, William H. *All about Coffee*
Van Doren, Carl. *Benjamin Franklin*
Watson, John F. *Watson's Annals of Philadelphia and Pennsylvania*
Wharton, Anne Hollingsworth. *Heirlooms in Miniatures*

Herald Tribune, Philadelphia, Pa
Philadelphia Evening Bulletin, Philadelphia, Pa
Philadelphia Inquirer, Philadelphia, Pa
Philadelphia Press, Philadelphia, Pa
Philadelphia Public Ledger, Philadelphia, Pa
The Pennsylvanian, Philadelphia, Pa
Magazine of American History
The American Magazine

www.carpentershall.org
www.philageohistory.org
www.philalandmarks.org
www.uphs.upenn.edu
www.ushistory.org
www.phillyhistory.org
www.nga.gov
www.curbstone.org

Bishop White House Staff
City Tavern Staff
Carpenters' Hall Staff
Ghost Tour of Philadelphia Staff
Physick House Staff
Powel House Staff
Josh Silver, who provided timely and efficient research assistance
Eileen Reeser, who researched and conducted interviews for
many of these stories

Old postcards of haunted Philadelphia

CITY HALL BY NIGHT. PHILADELPHIA PA

459 PHILADELPHIA—CONGRESS HALL, SIXTH AND CHESTNUT STREETS

INDEPENDENCE HALL, PHILA.

More Ghostlore at:

www.ghostlore.com
&
www.ghosttour.com